MUSIC IN AMERICAN LIFE

Volumes in the series Music in American Life are listed at the end of this book.

"My Song Is My Weapon"

Robbie Lieberman

"My Song Is My Weapon"

PEOPLE'S SONGS,
AMERICAN COMMUNISM,
AND THE POLITICS OF CULTURE,
1930–1950

UNIVERSITY OF ILLINOIS PRESS
Urbana and Chicago

Publication of this work was supported in part
by a grant from the Andrew W. Mellon Foundation.

Manufactured in the United States of America
C 5 4 3 2 1

This book is printed on acid-free paper.

Library of Congress Cataloging-in-Publication Data

Lieberman, Robbie, 1954–
My song is my weapon: People's Songs, American communism, and the politics of culture. 1930–1950 / Robbie Lieberman.
p. cm.—(Music in American life)
Includes index.
ISBN 0-252-01559-2 (alk. paper)
1. Music—Political aspects—United States. 2. Communism and music. 3. People's Songs (Organization) 4. Communism—United States—1917– 5. Politics and culture—United States. I. People's Songs (Organization) II. Title. III. Series.
ML3795.L44 1989
324.273'75—dc19 88-12226
CIP
MN

To my parents, Ann and Ernie Lieberman, for their love, inspiration, and encouragement, and to the memory of Dick Reuss, whose thoughtfulness and enthusiasm is missed by all.

Contents

I hate a song that makes you think that you're not any good. I hate a song that makes you think you're just born to lose. Bound to lose. No good to nobody. No good for nothing. Because you are either too old or too young or too fat or too thin or too ugly or too this or too that. Songs that run you down or songs that poke fun at you on account of your bad luck or your hard traveling.

I am out to fight these kinds of songs to my very last breath of air and my last drop of blood. I am out to sing songs that will prove to you that this is your world and that if it has hit you pretty hard and knocked you for a dozen loops, no matter how hard it's run you down, and rolled over you, no matter what color, what size you are, how you are built; I am out to sing the songs that will make you take pride in yourself.

Woody Guthrie, 1947

. . . the Communists everywhere are the only people I know of that know how to make the right use of our own American folk lore, folk culture, folk songs, and folk singers. And folks.

Woody Guthrie, *People's World,* April 28, 1947

Preface

What happens to a song after it is written? No matter what the writer's intentions, the fate of a song depends on political, historical, and cultural contexts that we understand most clearly with hindsight. No one guessed that Woody Guthrie's "This Land Is Your Land"—without the militant verses and spirit in which it was written—would become a national anthem for school children.

The reexamination of culture going on in all parts of the world today adds new dimensions to my inquiry into the left-wing folk movement of the 1930s and 1940s. Some of the problems faced by People's Songs in the 1940s are similar to those that artists and critics face today in China, Nicaragua, Chile, the United States, and the Soviet Union. For example, today there is a new openness toward art in the Soviet Union, where the official government policy of *glasnost* has unleashed much energy and confusion. Artists can experiment in literature, poetry, graphic art, theater, film, dance, and music. Soviet citizens can now read Boris Pasternak and attend a Marc Chagall exhibit. They can now see films that sat on shelves for twenty-five years and new documentaries that address such touchy issues as the war in Afghanistan. Musicians publicly call for more candor in rock lyrics and urge that young people be allowed to dance at rock concerts. It is unclear where this process will lead, but it once again raises intriguing questions about the relationship between art and politics.

In a broad sense, my concern here is with the political uses of art. My starting points are the large historical and theoretical questions outlined below. At the same time, the motivation for this study was not only intellectual, but personal as well. I grew up in the 1960s with many of the songs of the Old Left, sung by my father (a former People's Songster) at gatherings of family and friends. I also heard the songs on records and even on the radio, when some of them became part of the 1960s folk revival. I became curious about what these songs had meant to participants in the Communist movement and, in turn, to the broader American culture. What traditions had people who sang and wrote these songs drawn on; what had inspired them; why had they persisted? How could they continue to sing these songs with such fervor twenty and thirty years later, yet be so critical of the political movement that had nurtured the songs? Why did the older people I knew sing "Bread and Roses" and "Song of My Hands" with such passion and sing "Put It on the Ground" and "Friendly Henry Wallace" with a knowing twinkle in their eyes? The evidence led me to conclude that the politics and culture of the movement were inextricably linked and that this link was an essential, yet relatively neglected, component of the story of American Communism.

From 1946 to 1949 a small group of left-wing cultural workers organized to sing out for labor, civil rights, civil liberties, and peace. People's Songs, Inc., continued a tradition and left a legacy of protest singing that continues to this day. In spite of the organization's brief lifespan—indeed, in some ways because of it—the story of People's Songs provides us with a number of insights into cold-war America, the American Communist movement, and the experience of left-wing cultural workers.

The founders of People's Songs shared some distinct characteristics: youth, musical talent or interest, and a commitment to folk music and communism. Neither big names in show business nor political leaders on the Left, People's Songs activists demonstrated aspects of a rank-and-file commitment to communism which, until recently, have received little attention from scholars. People's Songs had no formal ties with the Communist Party U.S.A. (CPUSA). Individual People's Songsters—active members of the organization, many of whom were musicians—were not all party members. Yet the group as a whole was part of a broader Communist movement, an identification and commitment that account significantly for People's Songs' accomplishments and failures.

To illustrate this, one has to look at the variety of contexts that shaped People's Songs: personal (ethnic, religious, class backgrounds), socio-historical (the significant changes in American society brought about by the Depression and World War II), political (the communist movement), and cultural (the "discovery" of American folk music). The story here, then, is about the politics of culture of the Old Left, with special attention to the internal life of the movement (the "movement culture") and the use of song as a weapon. It is not about music per se, but rather about the attempt to use music for political purposes during a particular time period and within a particular cultural-political milieu.

The CPUSA was dominant on the Left in the 1930s and 1940s, until a combination of cold-war repression and the Communists' own sectarianism led to the end of the movement's political influence in American life. Its cultural influence did not end, however. For instance, the Old Left's use of folk music, focus on issues, hootenannies, and even specific songs ("Joe Hill," "The Hammer Song") helped lay the foundations for the culture of protest that developed in the 1950s and 1960s. My conclusion suggests some of the links between Old Left and New Left culture; the songs, singing, and issues that characterized People's Songs' work provided critical links between the radicalism of the 1930s and the civil rights movement and New Left of the 1950s and 1960s. When People's Songs dissolved, People's Artists continued its work, serving an increasingly isolated, sectarian movement. At the same time, the Weavers, a group with left-wing roots, achieved popular success singing folk-style songs, initiating the commercial aspect of the folk revival. Protest movements continued to rely on folk-style songs to express discontent and solidarity. A book on the movement culture of the New Left, with a focus on music, could treat fully the important and fascinating links between Old and New Left culture which are only suggested here. Coffee houses and college campuses, civil rights and antiwar organizing, Bob Dylan and Peter, Paul, and Mary—institutions, movements, artists that shaped the culture of a new movement deserve sustained attention, a book in their own right. But this book is about the movement culture of the Old Left.

People's Songs drew on the traditions of abolitionists, labor organizers, populists, socialists, and others who had used songs in their efforts to change the world. The organization was formed during a decisive period in American politics in order "to create, promote, and distribute songs of labor and the American people."[1] To this end People's Songs produced records, filmstrips, songsheets, and a songbook; staged concerts and hootenannies; and taught classes in the use of music for political action. People's Songs held one national convention, in 1947, and devoted a major effort to Henry Wallace's 1948 presidential campaign. At its height People's Songs had between two and three thousand members, with strong chapters in New York, Los Angeles, and Chicago. Its Board of Sponsors included Aaron Copland, Leonard Bernstein, Oscar Hammerstein II, and Paul Robeson.

In March 1946 People's Songs elected a National Board of Directors that included Pete Seeger, Lee Hays, Alan Lomax, Earl Robinson, Woody Guthrie, Bess Hawes, Millard Lampell, Felix Landau, and Walter Lowenfels. In October, Benjamin Botkin, Tom Glazer, and Waldemar Hille, among others, were added to the list; later additions included Mario "Boots" Casetta, Irwin Silber, Betty Sanders, and Sonny Vale. Pete Seeger was national director during the entire three-year lifespan of People's Songs. In the spring of 1947, as a result of attempts to base day-to-day activities on a more solid institutional structure, Irwin Silber became executive secretary, Waldemar Hille became full-time editor of the *Bulletin*, and Leonard Jacobson took over the bookings. After this the organization functioned more efficiently until a combination of financial and political problems forced its sudden dissolution in March 1949.

Their personal backgrounds help explain People's Songsters' passionate commitment in the face of the domestic cold war and the contradictions of the Communist movement. Some had spent significant parts of their youth in left-wing circles—at summer camps, square dances, educational functions, and political meetings. In such settings they developed their political outlook and creative talents, while finding inspiration in shared activity. In turn, People's Songsters were an integral part of the process through which the culture of the Communist movement evolved. This culture served as a powerful unifying force, simultaneously sustaining the movement and contributing to its isolation.

Maurice Isserman suggests that what sustained the commitment of Communists in times of crisis were the social bonds that united them. "They tended to live in the same neighborhoods, they spent most of their social life with other Communists, and their children played together. Breaking with the Party . . . would have meant accepting a status as a social pariah."[2] In a similar vein William Alexander, author of *Film on the Left,* claims that for some people the Left furnished a substitute family. "The attraction of people who worked together and shared resources in a common cause was immense."[3] Such statements suggest an approach to understanding the experience of American Communists that demands further development.

In his work on American Populism, Lawrence Goodwyn develops the theory of a "movement culture," which offers people hope and a vision of an alternative to the "received culture." The movement culture yields "a mode of conduct antithetical to the social, economic, and political values of the received, hierarchical culture."[4] While late-nineteenth-century Populism and twentieth-century Communism are not analogous—the latter was not a mass democratic movement—the concept of a movement culture illuminates many aspects of American Communism. The Communist movement culture, like that of the Populists, offered hope and a vision of an alternative social system to its participants. It played a critical part in building and maintaining the "individual self-respect" and "collective self-confidence" necessary to challenge the "received culture."[5]

Goodwyn's concept of a received culture is given more dimensions by Antonio Gramsci's analysis of the function of hegemony: "the 'spontaneous consent' given by the great masses of the population to the general direction imposed on social life by the dominant fundamental group."[6] Gramsci distinguished hegemony from "direct domination," in which the apparatus of coercive state power enforces discipline in moments of crisis when spontaneous consent fails.

In his elaboration of the concept of hegemony, Raymond Williams offers the following definition:

> It is a whole body of practices and expectations, over the whole body of living: our senses and assignments of energy, our shaping perceptions of ourselves and our world. It is a lived system of meanings and values—constitutive and constituting—which as they are experienced as practices appear as reciprocally confirming. It thus constitutes a sense of reality for most people in the society, a sense of absolute because experienced reality beyond which it is very difficult for most members of the society to move, in most areas of their lives. It is, that is to say, in the strongest sense a "culture," but a culture which has also to be seen as the lived dominance and subordination of particular classes.[7]

A lived hegemony, in Williams's theory, is a process rather than a system or structure. While the hegemonic is by definition dominant, it is neither total nor exclusive. "It has continually to be renewed, recreated, defended, and modified. . . . At any time, forms of alternative or directly oppositional politics and culture exist as significant elements in the society" affecting the hegemonic process. The Communist movement culture was in some ways such an alternative, in Williams's terms a "counter-hegemony."[8]

Much of the most accessible and influential work of the counter-hegemony, argues Williams, is historical—the recovery of discarded areas and interpretations that challenge the hegemonic's selective tradition. The activity of People's Songs may thus be classified in important ways as "residual," based on "a reaching back to those meanings and values which were created in actual societies and actual situations in the past, and which still seem to have significance because they represent areas of human experience, aspiration, and achievement which the dominant culture neglects, undervalues, opposes, represses, or even cannot recognize."[9] The movement culture addresses vital points of connection, where the dominant culture's version of the past is used to ratify the present and to indicate directions for the future. These are the points where a selective tradition is at once powerful and vulnerable—powerful because of its skill at making active selective connections, vulnerable because the real record is recoverable. "The residual, by definition," says Williams, "has been effectively formed in the past, but it is still active in the cultural process . . . as an active element of the present. Thus certain experiences, meanings, and values which cannot be expressed or substantially verified in terms of the dominant culture, are nevertheless lived and practiced on the basis of the residue—cultural as well as social—of some previous social and cultural institution or formation."[10]

Counter-hegemonic activity may also be "emergent," according to Williams. New meanings, values, practices, and relationships are continually being created. Emergent culture can only be defined in relation to a full sense of the dominant in order to distinguish elements that are substantially alternative or oppositional. What must be understood, says Williams, as a way of defining important elements of both the residual and the emergent, and as a way of understanding the character of the dominant, is that no dominant culture ever exhausts all human practice, energy, and intention. What distinguishes emergent culture is that "it depends crucially on finding new forms or adaptations of form."[11]

This mode of analysis offers insight into the Communist movement culture's challenge to the hegemonic process and, specifically, People's Songsters' promotion of traditional, rural folk music and topical songs in opposition to what they saw as a corrupt, mindless popular culture. Much of People's Songs' activity may be classified in significant ways as residual and/or emergent. Folk songs had been created by "the people," often in opposition to the dominant culture, and sung in forms that brought people together to form a community. People's Songsters saw themselves as both recovering a tradition and adding to it by writing lyrics that commented on current political issues and implicitly suggested visions of an alternative future. They also offered ways for people to participate in counter-hegemonic activity by adapting residual forms of singing—the hootenanny and political campaign singing—to their own purposes.

Songs and singing were important within the Communist movement and, indeed, sometimes reached people outside the movement. The composers and performers also merit attention because their experience challenges the characterization of American Communism as cynical, manipulative, and destructive. The latter view provides the framework for much of the scholarly work on American Communism, including the major book on folk music and the American Left, R. Serge Denisoff's *Great Day Coming!*[12] My analysis is based on a critical view of the American Communist movement, emphasizing People's Songs' connection to that movement, for better and worse. Yet I have avoided the terms "Stalinism" and "Communist front," used too often as abusive terms and as excuses to dismiss the work of the Communist movement as totalitarian, conspiratorial, and duplicitous. Such labels do not contribute to a balanced analysis of left-wing thought and activity, nor do they reflect how cultural workers such as People's Songsters viewed themselves. They did not identify themselves as "Stalinists" nor their organization as a "Communist front." Because the point of this study is to indicate the possibilities opened up by a broader approach to American Communism—focusing on the contradictory experiences and ideas of rank-and-file participants—I have found it preferable to avoid using terms that reaffirm a way of thinking that reduces Communists to either cynical manipulators or malleable objects.

In recent years scholars have begun to challenge the negative stereotype of American Communism, focusing on positive contributions to American life in such areas as labor organizing, civil rights, and the arts.[13] My own argument is that there is a significant connection between the failures and weaknesses of American Communism on the one hand and the contributions and strengths of the movement on the other. These contradictions and accomplishments simultaneously characterized, and became the legacy of, the American Communist movement. We cannot choose one and omit the other if we are writing a balanced history of American Communism, no matter on which period or group of Communists we choose to focus. The temptation in my own study is to simply condemn the political style and mistakes of the American Communist movement while praising its cultural contributions. Yet this would be missing the point. Without the wholeness and quality of the movement's internal life, sectarianism and lack of democracy notwithstanding, the depth of commitment that led to significant creative work would have been lacking. While their commitment to the Communist movement drastically limited the impact of People's Songsters—because of domestic anticommunism and the American movement's subordination to Soviet Communism—the same passionate commitment explains their positive contributions to American life.

Beyond the question of the political and cultural legacy of American Communism, what is at stake here are issues concerning the role of culture in constituting people's lives and world views. Debate continues about how important the cultural realm really is in the process of challenging hegemony and achieving social change. This is where focusing on the movement culture has distinct advantages over previous approaches to the study of American Communism. Manipulation, corruption, and betrayal—explanations that characterize much of the scholarship on the subject—give way to emphasis on how a variety of forms of domination are experienced, internalized, and challenged. Cultural activity is also extended a more central role in expressing and constituting people's sense of reality. Cultural expressions, as Williams argues, are related to "a wider area of reality than the abstractions of 'social' and 'economic' experience." Cultural work and activity are elements of a hegemony which "to be effective has to extend to and include, indeed to form and be formed from, this whole area of lived experience."[14]

Yet even if we agree on the significance of culture, we are left with numerous unanswered questions about the politics of culture in our own time. What is the best way to reach people with an alternative political message? What is the relationship between form and content? What meaning do the old songs have today? Who has access to the means of cultural production and in particular to the mass media? Do audiences simply consume passively what is presented to them as culture? To what extent are creativity and participation part of cultural life? People's Songsters' outlook and experience hold some interesting lessons for us here.

In addition to insights drawn from contemporary cultural theory and primary sources from the 1930s and 1940s *(New Masses, Daily Worker, People's Songs Bulletin)*, my analysis relies on personal interviews. I interviewed influential members of People's Songs, from its founders in New York and Los Angeles (the most active branches) to writers, performers, and organizers; from the editor of the *People's Songs Bulletin* to those who subscribed to it. I also talked with people who were active in the Communist movement at the time but had no direct connection to People's Songs. These interviews were an invaluable source of information about people's backgrounds and perceptions of their own activity. They do not always provide the "facts" more accurately than other sources, but there is no better way to ascertain the social meaning of experience, which must then be evaluated.

A number of people made this study possible. Richard Reuss and David Dunaway generously made available sources which would have been inaccessible otherwise. Richard Reuss also took the time and interest to provide valuable criticism in the early stages. Rich Crawford, John King, Jackson Lears, and Alan Wald also offered criticism and support when this study was in the dissertation stage. Alan Wald deserves particular thanks for incisive criticism, helpful suggestions, and necessary encouragement.

I made use of primary sources in a number of cities. A travel grant from the University of Michigan's Horace H. Rackham School of Graduate Studies helped make possible this aspect of my research. The staff of the following libraries and collections deserve thanks for helping me locate sources: Archives of Labor History and Urban Affairs, Wayne State University, Detroit; Archive of Folk Culture, Library of Congress, Washington, D.C.; Labadie Collection, University of Michigan, Ann Arbor; John Edwards Memorial Foundation Collection, University of California, Los Angeles; Woody Guthrie Collection, New York.

I am extremely grateful to all the people who responded to letters and/or granted personal interviews. For sharing their time and thoughts with me, warm thanks to Jackie Gibson Alper, Mario Casetta, Barbara Dane, Ben Dobbs, Frank Fried, Ronnie Gilbert, Frank Hamilton, Dorothy Healey, Fred Hellerman, Waldemar Hille, Harold Leventhal, Ernie Lieberman, Earl Robinson, David Sear, Pete Seeger, Art (and Alan) Shields, Irwin Silber, and Jerry Silverman. I gained many important insights from my contact with these people. My hope is that this study, in return, offers them new insights into their own experience.

Finally I would like to thank Judith McCulloh and Archie

Green for believing in this project and encouraging me to do it well; Bill Loizeaux and Pete Seeger for their comments on earlier drafts; Chris D'Arpa and Aletta Brink for last-minute research assistance; Ann and Ernie Lieberman for their neverfailing support; and last, but not least, Rich Fedder for his enormous supply of patience, love, and encouragement.

"My Song Is My Weapon"

Introduction: Historical Background

As the Depression brought social and economic breakdown to the United States, the Communist International claimed that the crisis of capitalism justified a stage of revolutionary offensive on the part of Communists worldwide. Along with the belief that the collapse of capitalism was imminent, "Third Period" Communism saw the Soviet Union as the model for the creation of worldwide revolutionary socialism (a tenet that never changed) and expected that the Depression would lead workers to a revolutionary consciousness. In the United States this translated into a policy of organizing workers into dual unions to combat the conservatism of the American Federation of Labor and organizing the jobless into unemployed groups. The CPUSA also began to stress immediate problems faced by blacks. For example, the party defended the Scottsboro boys, nine black youths accused of raping two white women in Scottsboro, Alabama. Although Communism became a significant force among blacks during the period, Third Period labor policies failed miserably. However, contrasting the widespread unemployment, despair, and labor violence in the United States with the apparent energy, productivity, and hopefulness of the Soviet Union, many intellectuals turned to the Communist movement during this period. Intellectuals were attracted by specific issues, such as organizing the unemployed and the working class and defending the Scottsboro boys, and also by the sense of certainty, importance, and self-sacrifice that American Communism offered.

In 1935, at the Seventh World Congress of the Communist International, Georgi Dmitrov announced a new policy: Communists everywhere were called upon to abandon temporarily their goal of a revolutionary conquest of power and join with socialists, trade unionists, and liberals in a broad "people's front." Liberals and progressives who had been attacked as "social fascists" (for misleading the potentially revolutionary workers) during the Third Period were now desired as allies in the struggle to defend democratic rights. International Communism's major concern became the pursuit of a collective security pact between the Soviet Union and the Western democracies that would isolate the Nazis. This translated into domestic "Popular Front" coalitions promoting democracy and the broadest possible unity to defeat fascism. For the Communists, the Spanish Civil War became the testing ground and the symbol of antifascist unity. Communists from many countries lost their lives fighting against Franco's forces in Spain, and the songs of the Spanish Civil War continued to have tremendous emotional significance to Communists everywhere.[1]

Some Communists later claimed that the Popular Front had been in the making since Hitler's seizure of power in January 1933. Al Richmond was convinced that Dmitrov's report to the congress "articulated thoughts and conclusions of millions on the Left, Communists and non-Communists, all over the world."[2] Irving Howe and Lewis Coser suggest that the proposal for a common front against the Nazis would have been politically popular in the United States even without the Communists. Still, as they demonstrate, "the particular shape and tone that the Popular Front movement took in the United States was largely the work of the Communists. It was they who gave it coherence and expression, who inspired its activities and formulated its slogans."[3]

Whether one views the Popular Front concept as sound and valid or as the height of Stalinist manipulation and cynicism, the most striking point is its apparent success in the United States. Even its critics acknowledge that "it was the first approach the CP had found that enabled it to gain a measure of acceptance, respectability, and power within ordinary American life."[4] The acceptance and influence made possible by the Popular Front generated tremendous inspiration and excitement within the American Communist movement. The Popular Front meant new coalitions, mass organizations, and rhetoric as Communists turned to supporting Roosevelt and the New

Deal, building the Congress of Industrial Organizations (CIO), extending civil rights, and aiding the Spanish Loyalists. By 1939 the CPUSA boasted eighty- to ninety-thousand members and unprecedented influence in government, labor, black, youth, cultural, and other organizations. Yet beneath its apparent strength, the Communist movement retained significant internal weaknesses.[5]

The contradictions of the Communists' Popular Front politics are glaring in retrospect. For example, the concern with *Soviet* security led to a focus on extending *American* democracy; at the same time, the emphasis on democracy did not include the movement itself. There was no internal debate about party policy. As Dorothy Healey says, "Whatever it was it was right for the period."[6] The work of Communists in the CIO, in Spain, in Harlem, and elsewhere was undercut by the internal process of the movement, which contradicted its own rhetoric and achievements. Communist internationalism provides one example of how the movement's internal rigidity undermined its external achievements. The Communists' opposition to the rise of fascism, as expressed in the focus on Spain and the individual heroism of those who fought in the Lincoln and International brigades, was exemplary and inspirational. On the other hand, Communist internationalism also meant that the primary concern was the defense of the Soviet Union, a perspective which allowed many people to accept the Moscow trials at face value or to abruptly change their position on the war after the Nazi-Soviet pact. This ambiguity applied to domestic issues as well. For example, pioneering work with labor and civil rights groups was undermined by the Communists' lack of independence and their inability to reject sectarian policies that contradicted their own instincts and experience.[7]

The democratic spirit that defined Popular Front Communism in the U.S. turned out to be temporary. It was abruptly discarded, no longer deemed appropriate, when Stalin signed the nonaggression pact with Hitler in 1939. The movement declined rapidly in some areas during the period between the signing of the pact on August 22, 1939, and the German invasion of Russia on June 22, 1941. Popular Front organizations dissolved, while party membership and intellectual support decreased significantly. Perhaps more striking, however, is the number of people who remained loyal to the movement in spite of the sequence of events during these years.[8]

There was some truth, however unintended, to the Communists' awkward public claims that their new policies were consistent with those of the preceding years. The source of the new line and the style in which it was handed down were consistent. Steve Nelson, among other participants from the time, makes this point in his discussion of the movement's reaction to the pact. There was little debate on any level about what direction the American movement should take. "Most people either fell into the groove or left," says Nelson. Falling into the groove meant defending the Soviet Union's actions and characterizing the war as an imperialist war. "It wasn't that we hated fascism any less," says Nelson, "but people saw us as mechanical pawns of Soviet foreign policy."[9]

Placing the interests of the Soviet Union first was hardly a new feature of American Communism. Even so, given the sequence of events from 1939 to 1941, the extent to which Communists had to rely on faith rather than critical thinking in order to remain loyal to the movement reached new heights. The pact, followed by the division of Poland and the Soviet invasion of Finland, forced American Communists to adopt "a kind of willing suspension of disbelief" in order to carry on their campaign against what they called the "second imperialist war."[10]

Domestic events compounded the confusion. In 1939 and 1940 Communists reacted to political harassment and a Red scare by taking measures to protect the movement's security and by setting up an underground apparatus. (This in turn reinforced the arguments of those who sought to portray Communism as a subversive conspiracy rather than a legitimate political movement.) Though the Communists took caution to maintain ties with the labor movement—for example, by supporting the CIO's anti-Communist resolutions in 1939–40—they could not convincingly argue with the perception that they were mechanical pawns of Soviet foreign policy. Strong public anti-Communist sentiment continued in 1941, after the legal attacks had tapered off, and was kept alive by accusations of Communist sabotage as a wave of strikes hit the defense industries. There was and is no evidence to substantiate the charges that the Communists fomented the defense strikes. Yet the Communists were vulnerable to these charges because their loyalty to the Soviet Union clearly came first in determining their policies.[11]

No independent political assessment preceded or resulted from the pact period. Dedicated Communists followed the CP leadership uncritically. John Gates explained the Communists' consistent support of the Soviet Union as the bulwark of a world movement and their acceptance of strategy worked out by others: "It is true that we were never consulted on the world strategy of which we assumed ourselves a part and by which we were governed . . . we saw it as the only possible strategy since those who had worked it out were assumed to be the wisest of all Communists."[12] George Charney put it more succinctly: "Our faith held."[13]

When Germany attacked the Soviet Union in 1941, the Communists changed their line again. Their support of American participation in the "people's war" to defeat fascism brought Communists to their peak of popularity in the United States. The new line, which combined defense of the Soviet Union with loyalty to the United States, generated tremendous excitement within the movement. Its popularity made it easy to overlook the style in which the new line was implemented—as usual, from the top down. The Communists' new policy was not simply a return to the Popular Front. The defense of the Soviet Union demanded that the first priority be American participation in the war to defeat Hitler. Especially after Pearl Harbor, this meant that "anything that had to be done to ensure victory was acceptable."[14]

As the movement changed its tactics in various arenas in order to concentrate on the war effort, Communist militance took a back seat. The struggle for black rights, for example, in which Communists had played a leading role in the 1930s, was limited to those areas in which the war effort was believed to be affected. The Communists had attacked the March on Washington Movement, which pressured FDR into creating a Fair Employment Practices Committee, as being too bourgeois in 1941. In 1942 they opposed it on the grounds that it was too militant. Yet they carried on an important battle in unions, such as the National Maritime Union, for equal employment rights for blacks. As Maurice Isserman argues, the Communist movement narrowed, but did not abandon, the struggle for black rights. In

Harlem, for instance, "The Communists reached the highwater mark of their political influence . . . during the very years when, if the conventional account was true, they logically ought to have been losing strength."[15]

The Communists also abruptly curbed the labor militance that had characterized their role in building the CIO. They supported the no-strike policy and the measures of the War Labor Board in order to guarantee uninterrupted production of war materials, and they downplayed class conflict. The editors of *New Masses*, responding to an attack on American capitalism by Upton Sinclair, stated that "the majority of American capitalists today recognize fascist Germany and Japan as a menace to our national independence without which their own independent functioning would become impossible. That is why these capitalists, in contrast to the defeatist minority, want America to win and have joined with other classes and groups to assure victory. To raise other issues at this time, issues that accentuate conflicts between capital and labor, does not, it seems to us, contribute to the strengthening of that unity for war and peace which Mr. Sinclair urges."[16] Communists did not lose their hopes for the long-term prospects for progressive unionism, but their outlook and policies actually served to strengthen conservative trends in the labor movement.

In addition, the Communists changed their electoral tactics. They ran no candidates of their own in 1944, having dissolved the party in May, yet they made the most concerted electoral effort in their history that year. The Communists became convinced that they were desirable political allies when their participation in the CIO Political Action Committee contributed to Roosevelt's reelection.[17] The campaign also provided them with experience which would come in handy during the 1948 Progressive party campaign for Henry Wallace.

In the short run, the Communist movement regained its prewar strength, while increasing the proportion of party members who were blacks and industrial workers. In the long run, the Communists' failure to learn important lessons from the war experience increased the speed and depth of their postwar decline. But during the war the emphasis on domestic and international cooperation brought the Communists unprecedented popularity. The Teheran meetings in 1943, at which Roosevelt, Churchill, and Stalin pledged that their nations would work together in war and peace, fueled the hopes for postwar unity. Earl Browder, then the leader of the American Communist party, may have gone further than anybody in his enthusiasm for the spirit of Teheran, but he was not alone in his hopes that the agreement presaged lasting peace and international cooperation.[18]

President Truman's decision to drop two atomic bombs on Japan and hasten the end of World War II signaled for many the end of wartime optimism. A letter to the editor of *Time* magazine summed up the feeling that the world had changed dramatically: "We have this day become the new master of brutality, infamy, atrocity. . . . No peacetime application of this Frankenstein monster can ever erase the crime we have committed. . . . It is no democracy where such an outrage can be committed without our consent."[19]

There is no little irony in the perception shared by American historians that the "crisis" of the 1940s was not World War II itself but rather the years immediately following the war. On the surface U.S. participation in the war seemed to resolve the most serious domestic problems, especially economic ones. Military spending led to expanded manufacturing, higher levels of employment, a growing GNP, and higher standards of living for many people. Geoffrey Perrett lauds the war experience for coming "as close as this country has ever come to living the American Dream." On the surface, the war also brought a sense of unity to the nation. There was popular support for the war effort; people cooperated in a shared purpose; some groups, notably blacks and women, found opportunities for mobility, employment, and participation that had not existed prior to the war. Yet it is facile to conclude from this that "a nation that stumbled into 1939 shaken, divided, confused, and unhappy" came out of World War II "strong, united, whole, happy, and confident."[20]

The seeds of reaction and postwar crisis that led to the *Shattered Peace*, *The Crucial Decade*, and *The Great Fear* were sown during the war itself.[21] It was clear, for example, that business and labor were headed for a showdown. Though unions made tremendous membership gains during the war, such measures as the no-strike pledge and a wage freeze prevented workers from sharing proportionately in the increasing corporate profits derived from war production. Concessions made to blacks during the war for reasons of expediency—such as the Army broadening its policy because of the need for manpower—did not lead to dramatic changes in their social position after the war. (There was intense congressional opposition to the Fair Employment Practices Commission, for example.) The government nurtured the military-industrial complex, while it abolished relief agencies such as the Civilian Conservation Corps and the Works Progress Administration.

National unity, sometimes expressed in an overblown patriotism and Americanism, led to violations of civil liberties. The most extreme example was the forced detention of more than a hundred thousand Japanese and Japanese-Americans in relocation camps. (Communist support for wartime relocation, and for the Smith Act persecution of Trotskyists, did not stand the movement in good stead when a few years later it was forced to defend its own civil liberties.) The obsession with "Americanism" was not a wartime aberration, but rather the beginning of a crisis mentality which reached new heights in the late 1940s and early 1950s.

The cold war itself was germinating even during the period of the Soviet-American alliance. The CPUSA increased its membership during the war years, while the Russians were admired for their heroic sacrifices in fighting fascism. In 1943 *Life* magazine published a special feature issue on the Soviet Union, praising its industrial, agricultural, military, and cultural achievements. Yet in the same year, talk of the "next war"—the anticipated fight against the Soviet Union—had already begun.[22]

Truman's succession to the presidency, following FDR's death in April 1945, led to the obsession with communism and disloyalty that characterized the postwar period. The crisis mentality that developed after the war was not based simply on economic and social problems such as prices, housing, employment, labor relations, and civil rights. To a great extent, the Truman administration created the atmosphere of crisis in order to gain support for its domestic and foreign policies. Industry's dependence on military production provided the economic basis for a permanent arms race and large military budget. Economic arguments were supported by a political rationale which emphasized Soviet threats of expansion. The national security doctrine was based on a new perception of the relationship of the United States to the rest of the world, in particular the view that the United States had to be prepared for a limitless range of military threats.[23]

Daniel Yergin argues that "the postwar anti-communist consensus existed first in the center, in the policy elite, before it spread out to the nation."[24] The House Committee on Un-American Activities became permanent in 1945 upon the suggestion of Congressman John Rankin of Mississippi. Winston Churchill's "Iron Curtain" speech in March 1946 pointed the way for American public opinion. Truman's loyalty program and the attorney general's list of subversive organizations contributed to creating an atmosphere of intolerance and fear. A state department report in February 1947, which found 70 percent of the public opposed to the "get tough with Russia" policy, was followed in quick succession by the Truman Doctrine, the policy of "containment," and the Marshall Plan.

Though the government dismissed or denied employment to hundreds of people considered risks to national security, federal loyalty checks in fact turned up few results. In 1950 the chairman of the District of Columbia Loyalty Board told a Senate committee that "not one single case or evidence directing toward a case of espionage has been disclosed in the record."[25]

The visible and dramatic anticommunism of the HUAC investigations and the Smith Act trials fail to suggest the scope of the purge that was eventually carried out on all levels of society. Local, state, and federal legislation and committees, as well as self-appointed vigilantes, harassed individuals, groups, and institutions. People were fired from their jobs; discriminated against in housing, social security, and unemployment benefits; and deported. Such actions were justified on the basis of past membership in allegedly subversive organizations, guilt by association, reliance on the Fifth Amendment, and refusal to cooperate with congressional committees. Whatever genuine crisis existed was translated into a nationwide sense of crisis in the form of widespread anticommunism.

As the government and the nation turned to the right, the Communist movement predicted economic crisis and the growth of militant class consciousness. The Communist International called for an offensive against U.S. imperialism, and American Communists became convinced that the United States was on the road to fascism. The immediate signal for American Communism's left turn was the Duclos article, a message from Moscow printed in the French Communist party's theoretical journal *Cahiers du Communisme.* The article criticized CPUSA general secretary Earl Browder's revisionism, "expressed in the concept of a long-term class peace in the U.S." This set in motion the movement's repudiation of "Browderism" and its return to orthodoxy.[26] The American Communist movement's reaction to the Duclos article indicated that the movement's political perspective would continue to be defined by international events outside its control.

The combination of attacks from without and misjudgments from within spelled the end of the Communist movement as an influential force in American politics. The Communists' support for Henry Wallace's presidential campaign in 1948 was a desperate attempt to provide an alternative to the cold war and the national security doctrine. The Smith Act trials of the top CPUSA leaders began in January 1949. The party began to prepare itself for further tribulations by consolidating its ranks, engaging in its own internal witch-hunt against untrustworthy Communists, and sending its leadership underground.[27] At the height of the cold war, the Communist movement devoted much of its energy to legal and political defense struggles, while it carried on public activities on behalf of peace. A final attempt to reevaluate and democratize the CPUSA followed Khrushchev's 1956 speech in which he denounced Stalin. A group led by John Gates failed to convince the CPUSA to set its own independent course. By 1957 the Communist movement was a shell of its former self, surviving mainly in the form of ideals and symbols (songs among them) that had held it together since World War II.

Irving Howe and Lewis Coser's conclusion about American communism is that "in cultural matters as in politics . . . our story is a story of human waste."[28] Not only does this generalization fail to credit Communists for important work in labor, civil rights, politics, and culture, it assumes that the cultural realm was simply a reflection of the political line. The experience and legacy of many groups of American Communists, political and cultural, challenges Howe and Coser's conclusion. We now turn to an exploration of the movement culture to help explain people's commitment to a movement that was so often isolated by its own sectarian view of the world. Paradoxically, the demise of the CPUSA following World War II was matched by the tenacity of its movement culture, which songs played a central role in sustaining.

1

The American Communist Movement Culture

The quality of life on the Left is a compelling explanation for the passion, commitment, and failings of many American Communists. Steve Nelson explains that the Left in New York City "was isolated by its very nature. The viability of its radical subculture sometimes prevented it from spreading its wings and leaping out of the old familiar environment."[1] Understanding how the Communist movement culture defined the quality and meaning of its participants' lives helps us to see why People's Songsters and other leftists clung determinedly to their ideals in the face of the domestic cold war and the contradictions of the Communist movement. First of all, the movement was much larger than the CPUSA itself, including all those who shared the ideals of the party or were involved in its activities. Secondly, the movement culture was not the same as the movement. If the Communist movement is defined by those who carried on political activity guided by the CPUSA's vision or goals, the movement culture can be defined, by contrast, as a whole lived social process. The body of practices and expectations that supported the movement define the movement culture. The distinction is critical for analytical purposes. For example, certain features of the late nineteenth-century Populist movement culture, such as encampments and songs, outlived the Populist movement itself. These features kept alive meanings, values, and practices that challenged the dominant culture and that were inherited by the Socialists and later the Communists. In a similar fashion, the vision, social life, and songs of the Communist movement culture continued to show strength in the 1950s, even as the movement itself declined.

One did not have to be a Communist in order to adopt or maintain a left-sectarian world view in the early 1930s nor to experience one's connection to the Left as a defining aspect of life. Irving Howe, who joined the Socialist party in the 1930s, describes what it meant to be part of "the movement": "To yield oneself to the movement . . . was to take on a new identity. Never before, and surely never since, have I lived at so high, so intense a pitch, or been so absorbed in ideas beyond the smallness of self. It began to seem as if the very shape of reality could be molded by our will, as if those really attuned to the inner rhythms of History might bend it to submission . . . what mattered—burningly—was the movement, claiming my energies, releasing my fantasies. . . . The movement gave me something I would never find again and have since come to regard with deep suspicion . . . it gave my life a 'complete meaning,' a 'whole purpose.'"[2]

Though Howe makes such a statement in order to criticize such belief and devotion, his words reveal the power and importance felt by many people connected with the Left. For Communists, dominant on the Left at the time, the sense of possibilities and the feeling that history was on their side was all that much stronger. The Communists' sense of strength and purpose owed something to the wholeness of the movement—a wholeness expressed in concrete terms by an ex-CP member: "All my life . . . from the time I was fifteen years old, the Party was an enormous support system which came through in every crisis, political and personal, with love and comradeship. . . . And even beyond that, beyond crisis, it was a total world, from the schools to which I sent my children to family mores to social life to the quality of our friendships to the doctor, the dentist, and the cleaner. There was an underpinning to everything in our lives that affected the entire variety of daily decision, reference, observation, everything! No one who didn't live through it can understand what it was like or why it was so hard to give up."[3] Malvina Reynolds expressed the same idea very simply: "The movement was our community."[4]

In other words, the movement culture did not depend on coercion or direct domination to maintain its values. The power behind the movement culture was in some ways stronger than a threat of discipline or violence. Those who rejected the movement culture, having once been a part of it, were threatened with loss of meaning and community and the symbols, rituals, ideas, and commitments by which their entire lives had been organized.

Descriptions of the wholeness of life on the Left are compelling but not always representative. Some Communists led dual lives, keeping their work life and movement life separate. All Communists were exposed to the dominant culture, whether at work, at school, or in their neighborhoods. The pressure not to be a Communist was always present; confrontations with the values of the dominant culture were unavoidable. The wholeness of the movement culture could not prevent the tremendous turnover rate that characterized American Communism throughout the thirties, forties, and fifties. People left the movement for a variety of reasons. Political questions and differences drove people out at various points—over the Moscow trials, the Nazi-Soviet pact, Khrushchev's revelations about Stalin. Others were casualties of government coercion, such as victims of the witch-hunts in the early 1950s. At the same time, the party's own efforts to purify itself of untrustworthy elements drove others out of the movement. Some people adopted the values of the dominant culture after a few years in the movement. There were singers, for example, who were unable to reconcile their desires for commercial success with their connection to the movement. The careers of Burl Ives, Josh White, and Tom Glazer illustrate the difficulty of remaining committed to the Communist movement in the face of internal and external pressures to leave it.[5]

Even if the wholeness of the movement is sometimes exaggerated, it nevertheless was real enough to attract and hold many people. The Communist movement, similar to numerous sects that preceded and succeeded it, satisfied real needs. Especially for young people, it provided certainty and community. For those who "wanted to believe that there was an answer to the misery that was clearly around us," the movement provided that answer and more.[6]

The community created by the movement touched on every aspect of people's lives. It had its own labor fraternal orders, its own housing cooperatives, and its own summer camps, and all of these institutions carried on political and cultural activities. One example is the International Workers Order (IWO), a radical labor fraternal order founded in 1930 by left-wing dissidents from the Workmen's Circle. While its membership was not limited to Communists, the IWO's public positions were close to those of the CPUSA. The order sponsored fund-raising appeals for the Scottsboro boys and for training people to fight in the Spanish Civil War; it also expressed support for the Soviet Union. What attracted people to the IWO was its low-cost medical and life insurance programs and its active fraternal life. (Though the IWO became a multinational fraternal order, it was founded by Jews and it served as a central focus of Jewish Left subculture.) The IWO operated schools and summer camps for adults and children. It also sponsored lectures, classes, choruses, drama groups, and social events. As Arthur Liebman describes it: "The IWO provided a social world for its Jewish (and non-Jewish) members in which Communist and Left ideals were a central ideological focus. To the extent that IWO members could meet their social, cultural, and educational needs and interests within the order, they were insulated from contaminating contact with bourgeois social institutions, and their interaction with nonbelievers was limited. Immersion in such a social world . . . facilitated the acceptance by the members of Left ideals and ways of interpreting the world."[7]

A similar role was played by the United Workers Cooperative Colony, or the "Coops," a cooperative housing project built in the late 1920s in the Bronx. The Coops housed several thousand people, and the majority of the residents were Communist or pro-Communist. The Coops nurtured the Communist movement culture through activities and organizations, beginning with the Young Pioneers, a CP group that children could join at the age of eight. The IWO's largest schools were housed in the Coops. While some organizations were overtly political, cultural activities were also prominent, including choral, drama, and dance groups. Organizations for children and adults also focused on literature, science, or sports. All these activities had some radical political content. For example, choral groups sang left songs and Red Army songs. Athletic teams wore shirts with slogans such as "Free the Scottsboro Boys."

Liebman points out that young people growing up in this milieu learned to be proud, rather than ashamed, of their pro-Communist politics. They were conformists, not rebels or deviants, with respect to the value system of their social world. Reminiscences of Coop residents illustrate the point: "It created a sectarianism beyond belief, and a false sense of security for far-out ideas. . . . In a sense, it was an artificial island, an illusion to live here. You could make your whole life revolve around the Coops." Another resident affirms: "We in the Coops were convinced that we were the mainstream, and it was only after we moved out that we found what the real world was like." One resident reported having this dialogue at the age of five with a public school teacher: "'I see you live in the Coops. Are you a Communist?' 'Sure. I've been a Communist for a long time!'"[8]

Left-wing summer camps for children were one of the most important socializing institutions. Children who attended these camps were not all sons and daughters of CP members or Communists. Thus, for many people, summer camp was the place they were first exposed to or involved with left ideas and activities. Many campers became attracted to the Left as a result of their camp experience. Though the focus was on cultural activities, left-wing campers, counselors, and administrators set the tone at Camp Kinderland, Woodland, Wo-Chi-Ca (Workers Childrens Camp), and Unity, to name a few. The tone was distinctly Left, from the names of bunks and groups to the songs that were sung. Arthur Liebman interviewed one activist from a relatively apolitical family who traced the beginning of his involvement with the Left to his first summer camp experience at age eleven: "It had a profound influence on my life. I liked the way people related to each other. I liked the spirit that was involved. I became friends with the kids, a lot of whom came from Red families. I got caught up with them and then one thing led to another."[9]

Summer camps provided a congenial atmosphere in which leftists shared ideas and activities, and reinforced their beliefs, values, and political allegiance. Singing played an important role in this context, expressing and supporting left ideals. The camps were probably one of the most successful left-wing institutions, reaching more young people than did the schools of the IWO, for example, and making a positive impression upon them. While popular in the 1920s and 1930s, the camps became even more important in the 1940s and 1950s. As the Left became more isolated, summer camps became virtually the only place outside of their families where young people gained a knowledge of and sympathy for left ideas and traditions.[10]

In many ways the Communist movement culture took on a life of its own. But the point is not that children of the Left grew up so differently from their counterparts outside the movement. The movement culture—its beliefs and expectations, its vocabulary, institutions, and networks—contrasted with the dominant culture, but the process of socialization was very similar. Children growing up in the movement culture absorbed ideas that they did not fully understand until later in much the same way as did their nonmovement counterparts. Young Communists were neither brainwashed nor subjected to totalitarian discipline. Nor were they totally isolated. They played with the kids on the block, attended public schools, and were exposed to popular culture. Yet they grew up mainly within the bounds, or chose to become a part, of the Communist movement culture. From this culture they absorbed certain ideas, which they later accepted or rejected; this went for small and large ideas alike.

One significant example of the uncritical absorption of movement culture beliefs is the expression of blind faith in the Soviet Union. The notion that the Soviet Union—as the first Socialist country and the leader of the Communist movement—had to be defended against verbal and physical attack was passed on from one generation to the next. Communists refused to view the Soviet Union critically, no matter how much this refusal threatened their relationship with the American people. The extent of this faith in the Soviet Union is nearly impossible to conceive of in retrospect. Its expression is powerful testimony to the movement culture's internal cohesiveness and insulation. In discussing his commitment to Communism, Albert Maltz, who was a young writer in the 1930s, explained that during the Moscow trials "there were many like myself who believed that these people must be guilty, because we couldn't conceive that Bolsheviks who had fought together against the tsars and through civil wars could turn on each other and frame each other. This was inconceivable. I wouldn't have framed anybody else I knew. I didn't know anybody who would have framed me. We were starry-eyed and innocent."[11]

A youngster growing up in the movement—six or seven years old during the Moscow trials—absorbed unquestioningly the view of the Soviet Union's greatness: "We all believed in a better world free of poverty, racism, war and capitalism. The Soviet Union showed that it could be done. What the capitalistic press said about slave labor, secret police, Stalin, etc. was all lies. The Soviet Union was great and an example for all to follow."[12]

Similar ideas were expressed by others who grew up in or near the Communist movement and who became active members of People's Songs. Jackie Gibson Alper, born in Brooklyn, New York, in 1920, was one of three children of working-class Jewish immigrant parents. She says, "I cannot remember a time that we were not class-conscious or involved in some way in activities for the betterment of the community of humankind, both locally in our own communities and in relation to the nation and the world. . . . I was born into the left; I was a Young Pioneer, a YCLer [Young Communist League] and CP member, as I grew up and 'graduated' from one to another. Somehow my political activities always gravitated toward and included the 'cultural,' even as a child."[13] Alper joined and supported People's Songs from its inception and for a period of time worked in the offices of People's Songs and People's Artists. She also participated in musical, theatrical, and dance activities at concerts.

Ernie Lieberman also says he was "born into the left. My father was a member of the CP. My mother too. It was not spoken about as such. But we were part of the left culture: the books—from primers to Jack London. The meetings we attended—from when I was 4 years old. The songs I learned."[14]

Jerry Silverman, born in 1931, says he got a general political overview of the Left in the late 1930s as he was becoming aware of the world. His father was a big influence, both because he was active in the IWO and because he played the mandolin. Silverman didn't see music as a political act, but the two worlds overlapped. Silverman grew up in the Bronx, near the "Coops," and says that his whole social, cultural, and political life drew its breath from that environment. There was a general feeling of a progressive movement, and music was a regular part of it. Though Silverman did not join left-wing organizations as such, he says "I think it was all one left-wing circle, without realizing it. It was just so much part of the air you just assumed that's how life had to be."[15]

Ronnie Gilbert was born in 1926 to immigrant parents. Her father was from the Ukraine, her mother from Warsaw. Gilbert grew up with a strong union background: "It was a question of whether we had food on the table," she says. Her mother worked in a garment factory, was a member of the ILGWU, and sang in a Jewish Bund chorus. She also brought home the IWW songbook. Says Gilbert: "I grew up with those songs. We used to sing them together. And we used to march in the May Day parade. . . . That was the beginning for me, in childhood, and it was a very organic part of our lives."[16]

Fred Hellerman, who became a People's Songs performer and then a member of the Weavers, says he was "a Depression kid from Brooklyn." Born in 1927, Hellerman says one of his first memories is hearing kids chanting "Herbert Hoover, rah rah rah, stick him in the ashcan, ha ha ha." While his family was not particularly political, the atmosphere of 1930s Brooklyn was highly political. Hellerman says you just couldn't help seeing cans, money being collected for Spain, anti-Hitler rallies just everywhere. Hellerman became involved with the Left during his early high school days, started playing guitar while in the service, and began to sing more seriously after the war.[17]

Irwin Silber, born in 1925, says his parents became radicalized as he was growing up; his mother joined the CP in the mid-1930s. He was influenced by his mother and by his experiences at a left-wing children's camp. Silber says he was "a kid on the block" until the age of fifteen, when he became more involved in left circles. His cultural activities stemmed from his bent toward writing and his association with the kids at Camp Wo-Chi-Ca, rather than from any formal training.[18]

David Sear, born in 1932, had parents who were both political and musical. He describes his father as "a leftist until the Russians marched into Finland" and his mother as "a strong liberal." His father was a concert cellist and later a piano-tuner, and his mother taught piano. Sear was interested in both politics and folk music at an early age. Though he was never a Communist, he was part of left-wing political and cultural circles, from the Little Red Schoolhouse to Camp Wo-Chi-Ca. He worked with People's Songs nearly from the time it began, volunteering in the office and playing guitar and singing in all kinds of settings.[19]

Not all those who would become active, influential members of People's Songs grew up with the Left in the 1930s quite so literally. In that period it would have been impossible to foresee that a small group of musicians and organizers who believed in using folk-style song as a weapon would contribute so much to the legacy of American Communism. The group was not homogeneous in terms of geographical, class, religious, or political background. It included a significant group of New York Jews from working-class backgrounds who were part of the Communist movement culture from an early age. But the central figures in People's Songs did not all share these roots.

Earl Robinson (composer of "Joe Hill" and "Ballad for Americans") was born in Seattle, Washington, in 1910. He was brought up by a musical mother and started playing piano by the age of six. He remembers his father telling him that it was unfair for 10 percent of the people to have all the wealth. When he finished college during the Depression, Earl Robinson went to New York City and it changed his life. "When I came to New York, I expected to pursue my career at Juilliard or Eastman. I never did go to Juilliard. I went to Union Square and joined the singing movement, the left movement, the workers movement. Doing that was so much richer than any six Juilliards or Eastmans."[20]

Waldemar Hille (editor of the *People's Songs Bulletin* for most of its existence) was born in Lake Elmo, Minnesota, in 1908 and grew up in rural Wisconsin. His father was a minister who played the organ and violin and passed on an interest in music to all nine of his children. Wally Hille sang chorales and hymns in church and played the piano at the church school. His father was a German nationalist—pro-German in World War I and anti-Semitic—while his mother was more humanistic and progressive. His sister Marian strongly influenced his becoming involved with the Left. He lived with her when he first came to New York in the 1930s. He remembers hearing Marcantonio speak at a meeting for Loyalist Spain and thinking, "This is where I belong." He joined the Communist party soon after that.[21]

Pete Seeger was born in New York in 1919 to a New England "WASP" professional family. He was greatly influenced by his father, Charles Seeger, a musicologist who made the transition during the 1930s from an anti–folk song attitude to a concern with collecting, composing, and promoting folk music. Pete Seeger read Communist cultural critic Mike Gold's columns at the age of thirteen. He was conscious of the relationship between art and politics because of his reading of *New Masses*, to say nothing of family discussions at the dinner table. Seeger was an original member of the Almanac Singers and the Weavers and was the one person most responsible for the founding of People's Songs.[22]

Lee Hays, also an original member of the Almanac Singers and the Weavers, grew up in a conservative family. As the son of a Methodist preacher in Arkansas and Georgia, Hays became familiar with Methodist and Baptist hymns and with white and black folk songs of the rural South. His southern roots, his work with Zilphia Horton as a student at Highlander Folk School and with Claude Williams as a teacher at Commonwealth College, his unique singing voice, and his talents as a songwriter and songleader all added significant dimensions to the folk song movement.[23]

Mario Casetta was born in Los Angeles in 1920 to apolitical parents who were in show business; they did ballet and interpretive dancing in vaudeville when Casetta was a young child. He came to the Left through reading, curiosity, and most importantly through folk music. Casetta helped organize People's Songs on the West Coast and was the organization's only paid employee there.[24]

Frank Hamilton, born in New York City in 1934, also became involved with the Left by meeting people who were "folk singers and radical mavericks like me." His father was a socialist philosopher, and in part because of that heritage Hamilton was drawn to issues, rallies, and humanitarian concerns. But he was also drawn to "anything that had to do with folk music whatever and wherever. I want to believe Pete's [Pete Seeger's] view that the world can change because of a song."[25]

The younger generation of People's Songs tended to come from working class, left-wing, Jewish backgrounds. The "older" generation—with Pete Seeger at twenty-six and Earl Robinson at thirty-five when People's Songs was founded—came from more varied backgrounds. More significant, however, is that all these people had some connection with left-wing circles and institutions during their youth, whether or not they joined political groups. Whatever inclined these people toward the Communist movement, they came to be a distinct group. A sense of the world in which they grew up is suggested by this song, sung in Communist circles in the 1930s:

> Fly higher and higher and higher
> Our emblem is the Soviet star
> And every propeller is roaring "red front!"
> Defending the USSR.[26]

2

From the "Final Cornflakes" to the "Ballad for Americans": Communist Musical Culture in the 1930s

The CP's Third Period offensive in the political realm was complemented by cultural activities in the early 1930s, in particular the creation of "proletarian" culture as a weapon in the class struggle. Proletarian art in one sense was art created by, for, and about the working class. In a broader sense it was art created from a "proletarian" point of view, expressing a class-conscious radicalism. While proletarian culture could take many forms, the party's main interest was in literature, for a variety of reasons. Not only did the Soviet model hold sway in politics, promising full employment, productivity, and hope, but it also had an important influence in culture, promising revolutionary new content and techniques in the arts. In the Soviet Union, writers were a valued part of socialist reconstruction, and so they were highly respected by the CPUSA as well. In addition, writers had obvious practical value to the party, especially as journalists. Besides, party intellectuals seemed to have a bias toward "high culture."[1]

As part of the program to develop promising artists of the proletariat, the *New Masses* founded the first John Reed Club in New York in 1929. These clubs sprang up in cities across the country, to foster the creation of proletarian literature and a few years later to win over middle-class intellectuals. Joseph Freeman's introduction to *Proletarian Literature in the United States* expressed the Communists' enthusiasm about the weapon of proletarian art: "The workers and their middle-class allies, in their struggles against capitalist exploitation, against fascism, against the menace of a new world war, furnish the themes of the new literature; they also furnish the audience of the revolutionary theatre and magazines. . . . Abstract debates as to whether or not the revolutionary movement of the proletariat could inspire a genuine art have given way to applause for the type of drama, fiction, poetry, and reportage included in this anthology."[2]

Similar developments took place in drama. Theatre Union was founded in 1933 to demonstrate the efficacy of "theatre as a weapon." Its purpose was "to produce plays about the working class, written from the point of view of the working class."[3] The hope was to create a professional theater supported primarily by working-class organizations. Theatre Union's existence from 1933 to 1937 coincided with the peak period of the proletarian novel. Similar to literature, drama of the 1930s was more concerned with what it had to say—confronting the audience with specific social issues and political alternatives—than with the means of dramatic statement. At the same time, Theatre Union went beyond agit-prop, seeking out plays that were both politically aware and dramatically sound.[4]

Left-wing filmmakers were also affected by the cultural ferment of the period. Leo Hurwitz, a member of the Workers Film and Photo League, remembers his first viewing of Soviet films and the impact of the new content and technique in cinema: "They gave one a new way of looking at the world, a way of growing and working from that, and a way of giving specificity to the outlook and the growth. They made one believe the world could be changed." In *Film on the Left* William Alexander characterizes the newsreels produced by the Workers Film and Photo League as journalistic, strongly propagandistic, sometimes analytic, sometimes dramatic, often convincing, and seldom, if ever, profound. They have "a certain flatness," says Alexander, because of "an unexamined assurance that mere documentation would suffice to engage the audience—an audience that . . . was assumed to be at least potentially in agreement with the films' politics." In a statement that sums up the expectations of proletarian artists, Leo Hurwitz and Ralph Steiner encouraged their fellow filmmakers to make film that "can carry our revolutionary viewpoint to an increasingly receptive audience, one that is really moved because in the life on the screen it finds its own aspirations and struggles, its own failures and successes, its own truths."[5]

Proponents of proletarian culture tended to ignore its defects. Ideological purity and the subordination of aesthetic concerns to political ones certainly had a detrimental effect on some creative work. At the same time, the inspiration and commitment many artists discovered through their connection with a movement and a shared vision led to substantial artistic achievements. The legacy of proletarian culture and the notion of art as a weapon reflects this duality. Much art was created in which the purpose of reaching people was defeated by the dogmatic, sectarian politics that dominated it. On the other hand, many artists who began to confront urgent social issues and who were awakened to new themes—in particular the life experience and thoughts of working-class people—significantly affected the future of American culture. Questions of the social commitment and responsibility of artists became an accepted part of cultural life, while the themes addressed by artists and writers were significantly broadened.[6]

While the legacy of proletarian culture is mixed at best, Daniel Aaron's conclusions about writers on the Left hold true for other cultural workers of the period as well. We still need to recognize

> the vitalizing influence of the Left Wing intellectuals who stirred up controversies, discovered new novelists and playwrights, opened up hitherto neglected areas of American life, and broke down the barriers that had isolated many writers from the great issues of their times.
>
> We . . . can regret their inadequacies and failures, their romanticism, their capacity for self-deception, their shrillness, their self-righteousness. It is less easy to scorn their efforts, however blundering and ineffective, to change the world.[7]

As Aaron argues, the commitment of artists was based not so much on party orders as on a shared world view that set the tone for their work. "The writers who wrote about bread lines, for whom evictions were 'an every-day occurrence' and the furniture of the dispossessed 'a common sight in the streets,' and who described in novels, poems, and plays the economic and moral breakdown of middle-class families did not get their instructions from Moscow. As might be expected, they dramatized their private difficulties and expressed, often with more passion than felicity, their feelings of outrage at what they saw with their own eyes."[8] It was the human suffering of the Depression, and the sense that the Communists offered the only viable cure, that drew people into left-wing cultural activities and organizations. The Communists' analysis of society in the early 1930s gave meaning to the creation of proletarian culture. Artists identifying with the working class as the agent of an imminent revolution believed they were contributing to the creation of an exciting new world.[9]

Again, those who grew up in the Communist movement culture absorbed this world view as youngsters. Ernie Lieberman's earliest musical memory is being in left-wing adult camps and his mother singing to him to keep him quiet—mostly international revolutionary songs, Russian songs. From a very early age, he would be the one at campfires who knew the words to all the songs. He remembers singing the "Internationale" at the age of four, when the chorus began not with "Tis the final conflict" but with "Tis the final cornflakes."[10]

In the same year, 1934, the Composers Collective published its first *Workers Songbook*, with a foreword that proclaimed:

> Music Penetrates Everywhere
> It Carries Words With It
> It Fixes Them In the Mind
> It Graves Them In the Heart
> Music is a Weapon in the Class Struggle[11]

The collective was an offshoot of the Pierre Degeyter Club of New York City (named after the French composer of the "Internationale"), which in turn was an affiliate of the Communist-led Workers' Music League. The collective had about two dozen members, many of whom were products of traditional musical training at Harvard, Columbia, and the Juilliard and Eastman schools of music. Among the members were some of the most talented composers on the American musical scene, including Aaron Copland, Henry Cowell, Charles Seeger, Wallingford Riegger, Marc Blitzstein, Lan Adomian, Elie Siegmeister, Norman Cazden, and Earl Robinson.

Most of the collective's members were not Communists, but as in other fields of cultural activity, they had turned to the party for leadership in response to the chaos of the Depression. As Charles Seeger put it: "We felt urgency in those days. . . . 'The social system is going to hell here. Music *might* be able to do something about it. Let's see if we can try. We *must* try.' "[12] The collective set out to provide musical direction for workers' choruses in New York City and to produce and perform revolutionary music. Its work illustrates some of the problems inherent in creating proletarian culture.

The Composers Collective had a particular theory about how to use music as a weapon—a theory that grew out of their own experience and the character of the Communist movement in New York City. Their efforts to create proletarian music were shaped by their art music training, work with ethnic workers' choruses, and attraction to Communism. They expected to use their training to create mass song, to improve upon the "Internationale," for a revolutionary cause. The principal form of proletarian music activity at the time was the revolutionary chorus. In the 1920s this was largely an activity of the immigrant-language groups, mostly East European, which comprised the bulk of the CPUSA's early membership. (The best known of these was the Jewish "Freiheit Gesang Ferein.") These choruses performed doctrinaire, European-sounding songs, in foreign languages, based on music that was technically difficult to sing without rehearsal—qualities which began to concern Communists who wished to appeal to American-born workers.

Unlike groups in other cultural fields, the collective cannot be criticized for a lack of concern with aesthetics. Ironically, the particular aesthetic mode in which the collective chose to work made its compositions even more inaccessible than were proletarian novels, plays, and films. The collective's model was Hanns Eisler, a German revolutionary composer whose songs were sung in Europe by musically untrained workers on mass marches. Eisler demanded that songs be both politically and musically progressive. In the words of Charles Seeger, proletarian music was defined by its militance in text and tune, and by its association with the working class. It was to be revolutionary in content and nationalist in form. Workers needed their own unique music, free from bourgeois themes. Proletarian music would thus be "one of the cultural forms through which the work of humanizing people and preparing the proletariat for its historic task operates."[13]

The collective used classically derived musical forms in order to create mass songs and other choral and symphonic works. They viewed this as the best means of combining proletarian content with the "forward-looking technic of bourgeois art music" in which they had been trained.[14] They explicitly rejected native forms of American music—the IWW tradition of parodying hymns and popular songs, the New Theatre movement's use of popular music in political drama, the "hillbilly" music beginning to be heard on the radio, and folk music. Though radicalism and folk expression had met in rural areas of the United States in the late 1920s and early 1930s—for example, through Ella May Wiggins in Gastonia and Aunt Molly Jackson and the Garland Family in Harlan County—collective members did not view American folk music as a useful model for writing revolutionary songs. Carl Sands (Charles Seeger) wrote, "Many folksongs are complacent, melancholy, defeatist, intended to make slaves endure their lot—pretty but not the stuff for a militant proletariat to feed upon."[15] When Aunt Molly Jackson, the Kentucky ballad singer and union organizer, sang her songs at a meeting of the collective, Seeger said that the others were as unmoved by her fusion of traditional music with social protest as she was by their esoteric compositions.

The only attention the collective paid to folk music in its early years was due to its concentration on foreign models, particularly the "Mighty Five" Russian composers (Mussorgsky, Balakirev, Borodin, Cui, and Rimsky-Korsakov). Many of the Five's works were steeped in folk song, which led to the peculiar situation in which the Composers Collective attempted to write Russian folk tunes into American revolutionary songs. Only a few years later, the American Communist movement, and some of the collective members themselves, would begin to focus on American folk music as the basis of a progressive "people's music." The collective's songbooks gave some evidence of the shift. While there were no folk songs in the first, and two in the second *Workers Songbook* (from Lawrence Gellert's collection *Ne-*

gro Songs of Protest), plans for a third songbook, *Songs of the People,* emphasized labor-radical songs set to familiar tunes. Such songs were to make up nearly half of the book's contents.[16]

The strikes of the late 1920s and early 1930s produced mass songs which were parodies of widely known popular and religious songs and which were popular and effective in context. These included "Picket on the Picket Line" to the tune of "Polly Wolly Doodle," "The Soup Song" to the tune of "My Bonnie Lies over the Ocean," and "We Shall Not Be Moved" to the tune of an old spiritual. But the mass songs composed by the collective failed to appeal to a mass audience. As the collective composers became aware of their isolation, they began to use more familiar—and sometimes folk—tunes in their compositions. This process was described by Earl Robinson, who was heavily influenced by Carl Sandburg's collection of folk songs, *The American Songbag,* published in 1927. Robinson was unable to write a mass song until he took part in a demonstration. Even then he realized that it was only the Left that participated in singing "Down with Fascist Terror." Not long after this experience, he began to use and write singable tunes that went beyond setting slogans to music.[17] Still, it was not until the latter half of the 1930s, when Popular Front and New Deal interest in the American folk past coincided, that the Left began to promote folk music as a more accessible form in which to express revolutionary ideas. By the 1940s, former collective composer and theorist Elie Siegmeister could describe folk song as "the natural expression of our people who 'don't know anything about music,' . . . the deepest, most democratic layer of our American musical culture."[18]

The Composers Collective, which folded in 1936, left an enduring legacy for left-wing musicians to follow—a concern with the connection between aesthetics and political impact and particularly with making music accessible to large numbers of people. Its lesson, learned the hard way, is expressed in Charles Seeger's summary of his experience in the collective. Seeger's anecdote, as related by David Dunaway, concerns a 1934 competition for the best May Day song: "When the submitted songs were played through, everyone preferred Aaron Copland's setting of Alfred Hayes's 'Into the Streets May 1st' (with loud, rhythmic chords on the piano). Charles Seeger agreed that Copland's song was best musically, and his own much inferior. On the other hand, he pointed out, his entry was more singable. This was, after all, a marching song, and what worker could carry a piano with him on a march?"[19]

As Dunaway has pointed out, the Composers Collective was an unrecognized precursor—even if by negative example—of groups such as the Almanac Singers and People's Songs. Though the collective's musical interests and compositions differed dramatically from those of these later groups, collective members still shared a number of qualities with People's Songsters: musical talent and innovation, political commitment, enthusiasm, and hard work. The collective also shared with the next generation of left-wing musicians the sectarian world view that contributed to limiting its political impact. Despite the promise "not only to teach the masses, but also to learn from them," the Composers Collective and its successors fell far short of this desired exchange.[20]

Late in 1935 L. E. Swift (Elie Siegmeister) commented on "the comparative backwardness of proletarian music in this country as compared with the development of proletarian literature, theater, dance, and art."[21] While the Left was making creative advances in many cultural fields in the early 1930s, a viable left-wing musical culture, rooted in American folk song traditions, did not begin to emerge until the Popular Front was well established and did not become really dynamic until the 1940s.

The Popular Front offered an opportunity for the Communist movement to break out of its isolation and cultivate new friendships and alliances. For example, party chairman Earl Browder apologized to the Socialist party for the CP's past sectarianism:

> When we were singing that song "On the Picket Line," the most popular of our whole movement, there was that line: "If you don't like thugs and Socialists and scabs, come picket on the picket line." We have stopped singing that line of the song . . . but it still has too much influence in our minds . . .
>
> We should speak openly and frankly. . . . Let us admit that we sang foolish songs about the Socialists, that it was a bad mistake and that we cut it out.[22]

Browder's statement not only indicates a reaching out to former enemies. It also reveals the CP leadership's view of songs: songs were believed to influence people's thinking by reflecting and reaffirming the party line.

Browder embraced the coalitionist tactics of the Popular Front with an enthusiasm that horrified older, more orthodox Communist leaders. (It was this enthusiasm that contributed to Browder's downfall in the postwar era.[23]) But the broader ideological and tactical approach at the heart of the Popular Front was both anticipated and welcomed by young political and cultural workers. George Charney has described some of the feelings that accompanied the transition from Third Period to Popular Front politics. In mid-1934, Charney and a comrade had been severely criticized for preparing a leaflet that did not close with the party slogan, "For a Soviet America." Charney was dismayed: "We had simply written a down-to-earth leaflet which we hoped would interest the workers." His confusion over this incident contrasts sharply with his reaction to the Popular Front policy which, he says, "won immediate response among many union members, liberals, educators and others. . . . What could be more compelling during the crisis of the mid-thirties than the urgent call to submerge political differences in a common front against the fascist enemy?"[24]

Browder's concern with Americanizing the CPUSA struck a chord in people at all levels of the Communist movement. The party was restructured in order to conform to traditional American political units; party sections were reorganized along county and assembly district lines. Speeches referred to revolutionary heroes of the American past—Washington, Jefferson, Lincoln—and the American flag and the "Star-Spangled Banner" appeared at party meetings. George Charney and others who hungered for assimilation embraced the new Americanism of the movement: "It was as though a new day had dawned for the American movement. We were not only Communists, we were Americans again. . . . We were readily convinced that the two were not only compatible but inseparable. An American spirit began to pervade the movement."[25]

The CP's broad new spirit was evident in the cultural realm as well. The party's call for an American Writers' Congress in January 1935 was addressed to "all writers . . . who have clearly indicated their sympathy to the revolutionary cause; who do not need to be convinced of the decay of capitalism, of the inevitability of revolution." At this conference, writer Kenneth Burke received harsh criticism when he suggested that "the people" might be a more effective revolutionary symbol for the Communists than "the workers." In October of the same year, a call for an American Artists' Congress invited artists interested in "the objective of the preservation and development of our cultural heritage" and who agreed that "we must ally ourselves with all groups engaged in the common struggle against war and fascism."[26] Theatre Union, "America's one and only professional revolutionary theatre," folded in 1937. It was replaced by the Group Theatre and the Federal Theatre, which were concerned with social issues but were less dogmatic and revolutionary and did not offer specific solutions. The film collective Nykino had been working on "revolutionary films" in 1935, yet in 1936 it was devoting its efforts to the production of "progressive social films."[27]

The CP leadership's commitment to proletarian culture gave way to an interest in mass culture, with a focus on Broadway, Hollywood, and big-name writers who endorsed antifascism. A more significant aspect of the Popular Front approach to culture in the long run was that Communists became interested in folk culture. One panel of the 1939 Writers' Congress included Aunt Molly Jackson, Earl Robinson, Alan Lomax, and B. A. Botkin. Botkin spoke of what the writer had to gain from folklore: "He gains a point of view. The satisfying completeness and integrity of folk art derives from its nature as a direct response of the artist to a group and group experience with which he identifies himself and for which he speaks." Botkin called on writers to utilize folklore in order to "make the inarticulate articulate and above all, to let the people speak in their own voice and tell their own story."[28] At another session Lawrence Gellert, Langston Hughes, Melville J. Herskovits, and Alain Locke spoke of the importance of the Negro's* contributions to the national culture; Gellert focused on his collection of *Negro Songs of Protest*. The final Writers' Congress in 1941 featured a lengthy session devoted to poetry, songwriting, and

* "Negro" was the accepted term used by the Left at the time.

folksinging. Participants included Burl Ives, the Almanac Singers, Earl Robinson, Leadbelly, and Josh White. According to some accounts, this session evolved into a hootenanny, a format that became more common during the 1940s.

The movement's transition from an interest in proletarian music to an interest in folk music was anticipated and encouraged by Communist cultural critic Mike Gold. The shift was marked by Gold's review of the songs of Ray and Lida Auville, southern mountain ballad singers. Gold compared the Auvilles' songs with the work of the Composers Collective, finding the music of the former more valuable and progressive: "Not to see what a step forward it is to find two native musicians of the American people turning to revolutionary themes, converting the tradition to working class uses, is to be blind to progress." Gold went on to challenge the collective to learn from the Auvilles: "They write catchy tunes that any American worker can sing and like, and the words of their songs make the revolution as intimate and simple as 'Old Black Joe.' Is that so little?"[29] Gold's plea for art rooted in the American vernacular and his call for a "Communist Joe Hill" began to find a response in the mid-1930s. One month after his *Daily Worker* review of the Auvilles, the Workers' Music League dissolved, to be replaced by the American Music League. The goals of the new organization included collecting, studying, and popularizing American folk music.

The American Music League encouraged the use of folk songs in a formal context, true to its roots in the old foreign-language workers' choruses. While revolutionary choruses still held to a formal, classically based performance style, these choruses now began to perform in English and many more of their songs were American. The repertoire of the American People's Chorus, conducted initially by Earl Robinson, consisted entirely of American songs arranged in fine-art style. Such choruses helped popularize folk songs in left-wing circles and began to involve the audience more in participatory singing. But in the long run their impact was not as great as that of the emerging folksingers, individuals and small groups, who began to promote folk songs in a less formal, and sometimes more authentic, style in the late 1930s. It should be noted, however, that even as the Left's interest in folk music grew, New York audiences continued to prefer the smooth and polished sound of interpreters of folk music (Burl Ives and Josh White) to the raw and harsh sound of more "authentic" folksingers (Leadbelly, Aunt Molly Jackson, and Woody Guthrie).[30]

The Left's interest in folk songs partly sparked, and partly coincided with, a widepread interest in collecting and preserving American folk material. There was unprecedented official support for the arts; culture was attributed a significance in American life it had not had before. The Federal Arts Project for writers, artists, actors, and musicians recognized cultural production as work deserving of payment and furthermore recognized artistic skills as necessary contributions to society. Combined with its support for experimentation in the arts, these qualities made the Federal Arts Projects, though a small part of the total WPA effort, "among the most exciting and controversial." The projects set an important precedent for government responsibility and sponsorship for "the full range of human needs."[31] Artists who had visited the Soviet Union and observed its state-sponsored cultural programs yearned for such support in the United States. The WPA Arts Projects, though far from offering comprehensive support for the arts, partially alleviated "the weight of the American burden, the difficulty of the artist's task in America."[32] Left-wing cultural workers found that, for the first time, they had the simultaneous support of the Comintern, the CPUSA, and significant sectors of the American government and public. Combined with left-wing artists' discovery and genuine appreciation of American folk life, this unprecedented support for cultural work made possible what Joe Klein has described as "one of the happiest, most accessible, demonstrative, and inspirational periods in American cultural history."[33]

Former members of the Composers Collective—Charles Seeger, Earl Robinson, Herbert Haufrecht—became deeply involved in the process of disseminating folk music. Charles Seeger's transition from an anti–folk song stance to his role as collector and promoter of folk music represents a similar development within the Communist movement as a whole. (It was no coincidence that Charles Seeger's son, Peter, contributed so much to the popularization of American folk music.) Charles Seeger was exposed to folk music by Thomas Hart Benton (who performed folk songs in the early 1930s), by Kentucky ballad singer Aunt Molly Jackson, by George Pullen Jackson's book *White Spirituals of the Southern Uplands*, and by his association with folk song collectors John and Alan Lomax. He was also influenced by the isolation of the Composers Collective and the broad outlook of the Popular Front. In 1935 Seeger moved to Washington, D.C. to become director of the music program in the Technical Skills division of the Resettlement Administration. This emergency bureau, headed by Rexford Tugwell, was to assist with the relocation and social reintegration of communities uprooted by the Depression. Seeger planned to help reintegrate southern communities by organizing music activity based on the idioms of the people, which meant collecting rural folk songs.

In 1938 Seeger became assistant to the director of the WPA Music Project and, with Writers' Project chairman B. A. Botkin, organized a massive research and recording campaign centered on American music. In 1939 he published an article called "Grass Roots for American Composers," promoting folk music as the most important source material for composers: "The folk music of America [has] embodied for well over a hundred years the tonal and rhythmic expression of untold millions of rural and even urban Americans. Contrary to our professional beliefs, the American people at large has [*sic*] had plenty to say and ability to say it, so that a rich repertory has been built up—thousands of tunes each for the dance, for the ballad, the love song, and the religious song. . . . But American songs, hymns and dances were not, and still to practically all musicians and teachers, are not music at all."[34]

The work of Alan Lomax was even more influential in shaping the outlook of the left-wing folk movement. Lomax had begun to develop his ideas during folk song–collecting field trips with his conservative father. He was in a unique position to promote his theories in the Washington, D.C. of the late 1930s, where he served as director of the Archive of American Folk Song in the Library of Congress. Lomax encouraged a number of singers of American folk songs, from a variety of backgrounds, to perform in urban settings. These singers included Josh White, Burl Ives, Woody Guthrie, Huddie Ledbetter (Leadbelly), and Pete Seeger. Lomax helped such artists get bookings and an occasional record contract, hosted them on radio programs, taught them songs, and provided intellectual guidance.[35]

Lomax dates the beginning of the "folk song revival" back to the days of the New Deal in Washington. "The Roosevelts, the Tugwells, and the Hopkinses were interested in folk music," according to Lomax, because "they wanted to be identified with it as a democratic American art." They hoped it would promote cultural unity, giving voiceless groups "a sense that they, too, contributed very much to the building of America."[36] What emerged from Lomax's own work were precisely such New Deal and Popular Front ideas: a focus on American democracy which stressed the virtues of the common man and the dignity of oppressed groups such as the Negro, the functional character of folk song as a response to the particular experiences of American history, and the relationship of American folk song to its prototypes in the cultures of other nations. The major theme of American folk song, in Lomax's view, was "the theme stated by Burns's . . . 'A man's a man for a' that' and even more powerfully in the negro ballad 'John Henry.'" According to Lomax, songs such as "John Henry" linked "the races and the nations into the big family of humanity."[37]

The emphasis on the Negro's contribution to American life was central to the Popular Front ethos and the growing interest in folk music. Lawrence Gellert's collection *Negro Songs of Protest* became more popular. Some of the songs were performed regularly by left-wing choruses, some were interpreted in modern dance form in the successful production "How Long Brethren," and both collection and collector received more attention in the left-wing press. The movement press also began to pay more attention to black concert artists, such as Paul Robeson. The *New Masses* devoted much space to reviews of blues recordings, sponsored the widely acclaimed "Spirituals to Swing" concert at Carnegie Hall in 1938 and again in 1939, and consistently supported jazz as "progressive," folk-based music. The importance assigned to black music was also evident in the work of Alan Lomax, from his recording and promotion of black artists to his theorizing about the meaning of American folk song. Earl Robinson also pointed out that the biggest contribution to folk song came from the American Negro: "Their songs have everything, tremendous strength and power of image and purpose and longing, soft beauty, subtlety of idea, humor—sometimes all these elements in the same song."[38]

The seeds of a new aesthetic were sown during this period, an aesthetic that was broader in many ways than the rigid art music standards of the Composers Collective. Elie Siegmeister wrote that the composer's task was to break down "the age-old division between learned or art music on the one hand, and folk or popular music on the other."[39] Marc Blitzstein used show tunes as the musical basis for a popular political drama, "The Cradle Will Rock." Charles Seeger began to create new standards by which to judge music, cautioning his field workers in the Resettlement Administration: "The main question . . . should not be 'is it good music?' but 'what is the music good for?' And if it bids fair to weld the community into more resourceful and democratic action for a better life for themselves, their neighbors and the human race, then it must be conceded to be 'good for' that. The chances that it will be found good in technical and stylistic terms will probably be more than fair."[40]

By the late 1930s, then, folk music began to be promoted as indigenous, progressive "people's music." In contrast to proletarian music, created by professional composers for the working class, folk music was created by "the people" themselves. Folk music demonstrated that people were active participants in creating their own culture. It was accessible to people and did not require the training and sophistication that art music demanded. Earl Robinson emphasized this point in his 1939 speech before the League of American Writers, in which he suggested that writing parodies—original poetry set to folk tunes—would assure a mass audience. Robinson claimed that "if you choose a tune which is hallowed and sanctified by the people having sung it and loved it, then they will be interested in your words also."[41] It was assumed that folk music would appeal to the heritage of the audience, even if many listeners were not personally familiar with traditional music. In the view of such partisans as Earl Robinson, Alan Lomax, and Charles Seeger, folk songs and parodies, people's music with progressive content, could become a great weapon for the Left.

The slogan of the Popular Front, "Communism is twentieth-century Americanism," was taken to heart by cultural and political workers. It was in one sense merely a new tactic for reaching out to the American people, an attempt to counter the prevailing view of communism as a foreign movement and ideology. As Theodore Dreiser expressed it in a 1936 symposium: "The reforms and revolutions, the changes from capitalism to socialism and communism, are inevitable and inherent in the very nature of things; and if identifying these changes with this powerful emotional force of Americanism will make these changes and processes of adjustment easier for the great mass of people, and correspondingly easier to bring about, then surely the American radical movement should make itself as far as possible free of European associations, and as American as possible in terminology, leadership, and general form." In other words, Americanism was a useful tool in the inevitable transition to socialism. In the same symposium, Newton Arvin expressed a less manipulative vision of Communism as the natural outgrowth of Americanism: "The spirit of this [American] tradition seems to me to be a radically democratic and secular individualism, and, in that confessedly partisan sense, I should say that this spirit is more truly what one means by 'Americanism' than any other. Only socialism now promises to make possible a democratic and secular culture in which all individuals may be genuinely free and genuinely human, and far from spelling an abrupt break with the American past, it will to this extent be the only conceivable realization of it."[42]

Some of these ideas are illustrated by the "Ballad for Americans," a cantata written by Earl Robinson and John La Touche that made use of both folk- and art music traditions while synthesizing the patriotic, egalitarian, democratic strains of Popular Front culture. In the fall of 1939 Paul Robeson's performance of "Ballad for Americans" reached millions of listeners in a CBS radio broadcast. In the "Ballad," Robeson relates a progressive version of American history—emphasizing freedom and democracy—to a chorus that keeps asking him who he is. After explaining that he is all races, religions, nationalities, and occupations, Robeson sings in conclusion that he is "America." The "Ballad" was so pro-American that the Republican party had no qualms about using it at their 1940 national convention. *People's World* claimed that the "Ballad for Americans" had been hailed by millions as "the greatest American song," one that trade unions, General Motors, the Republican convention, and the man in the street could all embrace and claim as their own.[43] About the Popular Front slogan, "Communism is twentieth-century Americanism," Earl Robinson says: "At that time, I bought that. I believe it is implicit in the "Ballad for Americans."[44]

A romantic view of the American past and present permeated Popular Front culture, focusing on the people and their democratic traditions and heroes, the natural resources of the country, and the potential richness of life in America for every individual. The American land and people were glorified by the radio plays of Norman Corwin, the films of Pare Lorentz, the writings of John Steinbeck, and the ballads of Woody Guthrie. The Communist movement's attempts to be "American" sometimes took forms that seem ridiculous with hindsight, as in the Young Communist League's new recruiting tack on a midwestern college campus: "Some people have the idea that a YCLer is politically minded, that nothing outside politics means anything. Gosh no. . . . There is the problem of getting good men on the baseball team this spring, of opposition from ping-pong teams, of dating girls, etc. We go to shows, parties, dances, and all that. In short, the YCL and its members are no different from other people except that we believe in dialectical materialism as a solution to all problems."[45] Yet the spirit of "Americanism" did help bring the Communist movement closer to the American people in some ways. For young people in the movement, the broader approach to organizing had lasting effects. Young cultural workers in particular were profoundly affected by the increased attention to folk culture, the attempt to reach a wider political audience, and the emphasis on antifascism and democratic reforms rather than on Communism as such.

The activities and ideas that characterized Popular Front culture left a lasting imprint on those who would be active in People's Songs in the post–World War II period. The political context in which "the folk" were discovered, and the resulting impact on cultural developments, shaped People's Songsters view of song as a weapon. Composer and singer Frank Hamilton acknowledges the importance of the Popular Front in these terms: "The Popular Front was wonderful! It was because of it that I learned so much about music and society." Hamilton was too young, and at a later time too disinterested, to be in touch with the twists and turns of Communist party politics. Yet in retrospect he says: "Browder, as I understand it, was at the head of the Popular Front. He was trying to bring forth the goals of the CP by working with people antagonistic to the beliefs of the Party. This manner of working has always seemed better to me than attempting to establish an 'armed camp' of hostility. . . . Whether Browder was a great man or not, I don't know, but apparently through his efforts, I learned a lot about the Left."[46] Pete Seeger, who thought the speeches of Earl Browder made sense (even though he didn't understand them all) and admired people in the cultural field, claims to have been a "Popular Fronter" all his life. Earl Robinson claims to have reached a height of creative work during this period at a Communist-sponsored summer camp. "The summer camp brought together cultural workers with an audience in an atmosphere that stimulated both. Everything was educational and cultural. Songs like 'Joe Hill' were written to be sung at a campfire."[47]

Many people made their first connection with the Communist movement through culture. Ben Dobbs, who became a professional revolutionary, became involved through drama and remembers putting on a play about the Scottsboro boys with Will Geer. Yet Ben Dobbs can say, "I dropped out of the cultural movement when I became active."[48] By contrast, other young people in the movement did not differentiate cultural involvement from political involvement. It was all the same world to them. Young people were exposed to a political outlook and a style of music at an impressionable age. They embraced both the music and the politics, from then on viewing them as inseparable. Ronnie Gilbert went from being wrapped up in the Girl Scouts to the children's group of the International Workers Order. She began to develop her faith in the effectiveness of song as a weapon when she was strongly moved by the songs of the Lincoln Brigade—songs that led her to want to collect money for Spanish refugee children.[49] Jerry Silverman had his first contact with "people's music" when he heard Paul Robeson sing at a rally in support of the Spanish Loyalists. Irwin Silber remembers singing songs at summer camp—first Soviet songs, Joe Hill songs, and Spanish Civil War songs, and then folk songs from about 1939 on.[50]

Woody Guthrie was the major influence on those who began to link folk music with left-wing politics—an identity which young cultural workers absorbed as a given. Guthrie symbolized the potential for organically combining the music of the people with political concerns. Born in Oklahoma, Woody Guthrie grew up in the Southwest and migrated to California in the late 1930s. The Left in Los Angeles discovered him and encouraged him to continue composing socially conscious songs about the dust bowl and other issues. After writing a daily column in the *People's World* for six months, Guthrie migrated to New York in 1940. Alan Lomax recognized Woody Guthrie's uniqueness and worked at promoting his career, persuading Victor Records to produce his *Dust Bowl Ballads*, which were released in the summer of 1940. Though they would eventually be recognized as a landmark, the albums did not receive much immediate attention. Yet they were not completely ignored. As Joe Klein says: "The few copies sold seemed to be played continually—especially in left-wing schools and summer camps, where the words and the simple, defiant optimism became a part of the curriculum . . . as did the dusty little man wandering around the country with a guitar slung over his shoulder, making up songs that helped people to understand themselves and encouraged them to fight back. It was a powerful, romantic image, especially for kids growing up in the middle of New York City, and it would be central to the mythology of the generation of radicals coming of age."[51]

The reminiscences of New York youngsters support Joe Klein's claims about the importance of Guthrie's image and songs. Jerry Silverman says, "In my neighborhood nice little Jewish kids didn't study the guitar, and they didn't have Woody Guthrie and Leadbelly records . . . I did." Silverman evokes Woody Guthrie's image as a wandering left-wing bard in his remembrance of marching and singing in May Day parades at age ten or eleven. "I was not making a living or bumming around like my heroes. . . . I marched, came home and had chicken soup."[52] As a youngster Ernie Lieberman also idolized Woody Guthrie and went to see him perform. "Sometimes he didn't show up," Lieberman says. "It took me a while to figure out that he was a legend *not* because he disappointed people by not being where he was supposed to be, but because of the origi-

Woody Guthrie (photo by Robin Carson, used by permission. All rights reserved.)

nal music he was making." Lieberman describes one experience of watching his hero:

> One time he sang at a lodge of the Jewish People's Fraternal Order in Brighton Beach. It was a large, noisy room with people milling about and as much light on the audience as on the stage. When he was introduced almost nobody stopped what they were doing. The audience, aside from my young group, was mainly elderly, Yiddish-speaking, and interested in eating and socializing. Woody looked around and strummed his guitar. Nothing much changed. So he leaned back, closed his eyes, and proceeded to sing all twenty-four verses of "Tom Joad" (his dust bowl ballad of Steinbeck's *Grapes of Wrath*). He nodded to the few listeners and the slight applause and left the stage. We followed him as he picked up his $35 fee ("Wow, was he rich," we thought) and some of our brash, young group asked him for a treat when he stopped for a hot dog.[53]

The work of the southern labor schools also strengthened the link between folk music and left-wing politics. Highlander Folk School and Commonwealth College, in particular, played a significant part in the process of collecting, disseminating, and creating folk and folk-based compositions. Members of Commonwealth College in Mena, Arkansas, created union and other topical songs based on folk traditions—songs which they used in organizing in the surrounding countryside. Waldemar Hille spent time at Commonwealth College with Lee Hays, Claude Williams, and Emma Dusenberry, "making folk songs into progressive songs." As Lee Hays described it: "At Commonwealth, we were using songs in our own play productions and writing songs to order. We used a lot of religious material and stuff in the tradition of Joe Hill, and some other thoroughly original stuff. . . . Claude's [Claude Williams] influence was very strong and he sensed the importance of music. By then [1936–1937] we had already started singing "We Shall Not Be Moved," "Join the Union," and "Union Train."[54] When Commonwealth College closed down in 1940, Hays took the songs he had been collecting and developing there to New York to see if they could be put to wider use by the labor movement.

The Highlander Folk School in Monteagle, Tennessee, provided education and leadership training for workers. While its focus was on training union leaders to be more effective organizers, "singing together and giving plays had equal importance at Highlander residential workshops with courses on contract negotiation, parliamentary law, public speaking, or union problems."[55] Zilphia Horton directed most of the school's music and drama work, organizing group-singing sessions at workshops, teaching union songs on picket lines, and writing and collecting labor songs and chants that were used throughout the nation. In large part through her work, and the work of other students and staff at the southern labor schools, the practice of using folk music as the basis for union and other topical songs became a central part of northern urban left-wing culture, beginning in the 1940s.

Emotional and intellectual responses to folk music took place, then, in the context of the search for American roots, in labor organizing, in antifascist campaigns, and at left-wing summer camps. Perhaps the most important and lasting effect of the Popular Front in the cultural realm was the identification of "the folk" with left-wing politics, an identification that persisted both inside and outside the Communist movement. Though expressed in literature, film, and drama, this unity was nowhere more apparent than in the songs that began to be created and disseminated during the period. The enthusiasm with which various individuals embraced folk music and the extent to which they were moved by it in the context of Popular Front politics goes a long way toward explaining the subsequent development of the left-wing folk movement.

Pete Seeger exemplifies this process. He learned about folk music and left-wing politics during the Popular Front and has since been dedicated to creating and popularizing a blend of the two. Seeger joined the Young Communist League at Harvard in 1937. (He had had visions of becoming a journalist, observing rather than participating, but he later decided that this was a cop-out.) Seeger's outlook was also shaped by such experiences as attending a North Carolina folk festival in 1936, when he became excited about the five-string banjo; working with Alan Lomax at the Library of Congress in 1938; and traveling and singing with Woody Guthrie in 1940. From all this and more came his unique attempts to promote Popular Front politics using folk-style song as a weapon.[56]

Despite its relatively broad outlook during the Popular Front years, the Left remained isolated and insulated in many ways. Young people learned that serious political discussion was held most easily within the movement, among those who agreed with and supported one's views. For example, Pete Seeger found that he could not discuss in public what he read in the *New Masses*.[57] From inside the movement young leftists felt very powerful as they reinforced each other's ideas and commitments. Such insulation shaped the entire social life of some people. "I know," says one person, "that as a kid it was hard for me to *think* about being friends with somebody who didn't have a political indoctrination that was somewhat similar to my own."[58] In Jerry Silverman's words, "We were singing songs to each other. We were talking to each other."[59] The insulation of the movement culture clearly contributed to a distorted and sectarian political outlook, yet it also contributed to the hope and enthusiasm of youngsters who thought their broad, accessible approach could reach "the people." If one could not be entirely open about his or her politics, it was all right to reveal genuine excitement about folk music.[60]

The Popular Front left many American Communists with vague notions of what a socialist America might look like. Dorothy Healey, a union organizer at the time, summed up her vision during the period as "the fulfillment of democracy on every front."[61] For George Charney, the outlook was summed up by the phrase "through democracy to socialism," indicating the primacy of the defense of democracy over class struggle. "It was vague, of course, in terms of strategy and tactics, but it conveyed an altogether different image than the climactic and violent image of the barricades and 'the final conflict.'"[62] Ronnie Gilbert saw socialism this way: "It had to do with everybody working for a basic minimum guaranteed wage, so that nobody had to worry about clothing and housing and medical care . . . then people could turn their attention to how to make the products that they made better. There would be a decentralization of factories, and people would be interested in making the whole product. . . . There would be a constant educational program, and people would have an opportunity to change their lives when they discovered that there was something that they did better or wanted to do. There would be a lot of singing and painting and plays."[63] And probably only in the context of the Popular Front could the child who sang "Tis the Final Cornflakes" in the early 1930s have developed the following vision of American socialism: "When I was about ten years old, I tried to explain to the kids on Sterling Place about how the little candy store on the corner would be transformed under Socialism. It would be like a new gymnasium with soda water and syrup we could mix ourselves. And we could have candy and gum when we wanted it. And because we could have it we wouldn't overeat. And we could play basketball and punchball and whatever. I don't think I had a cohesive vision after that."[64]

Young people's understanding of Popular Front politics reflected the inherent contradictions of the Communist movement. They absorbed the party line, based on the defense of the Soviet Union, along with sincere concerns about democracy, antifascism, and the rights of workers and blacks. Only by understanding their interpretation of, and commitment to, Popular Front Communism can we comprehend the connection between their subsequent problems and accomplishments in the cultural realm. Michael Harrington has captured this connection in an impressionistic description of "the vision of the Popular Front":

> In it, one joined Spanish antifascism and the CIO and the black struggles and the New Deal and the Warsaw Ghetto and . . . the Soviet Union, in a gigantic confraternity of the overwhelming majority of mankind, which, if only given its head, if only freed from the plutocrats and fascists and colonialists, would rapidly and instinctively inaugurate a reign of human niceness. . . . There were many, many things wrong with that vision, and it was sometimes manipulated to rationalize cruelty rather than promote kindness. And yet, for all of its confusions and evasions and contradictions, if it was a corruption, it was the corruption of something good that always remained in it: of an internationalism that is still the only hope of mankind. I had read and internalized my Orwell; I knew the crimes committed by the GPU in the name of antifascism in Spain; and yet, I never cease to thrill at the songs of the International Brigade.[65]

The commitment of young cultural workers to a political movement that encouraged them and gave them a sense of security and power made possible their particular point of view—naive and sectarian, sincere and creative. In some ways the new Popular Front aesthetic was as sectarian as the "proletarian" emphasis of the preceding period. This is revealed in the emphasis on the revolutionary character of folk art and in the notion of "the people." The underlying assumption of the revolutionary purity of "the folk" and, by extension, their culture distorted the Left's outlook and expectations. Yet folk song, more than any other cultural form, expressed and reaffirmed the Popular Front spirit. It was simple and direct; it invited mass participation; it expressed the concerns of the common person. The popularization of folk music, especially in urban areas, had just begun in the late 1930s. Broadway shows, radio broadcasts, and concert performances exposed broader audiences to folk music. At the same time, the Communist movement was beginning to pay attention to folk music, absorbing it as an integral part of the movement culture. Left-wing experiments in literature, theater, and film ended abruptly at the close of the decade, with the onset of the war. In contrast, the folk song movement was only beginning to explore its cultural and political potential.

3

"This Machine Kills Fascists": Communism, Antifascism, and People's Music during World War II

The Communist movement shaped Popular Front culture in significant ways, providing the language in which many issues were framed and the symbols with which people identified. Communists were not the only ones moved by the songs of the Spanish Civil War; *Six Songs for Democracy* was said to be one of Eleanor Roosevelt's favorite records.[1] The American Communist movement had unprecedented strength at home in 1939. Membership in the CP and YCL was at a peak, and Communists controlled influential organizations of youth, blacks, and intellectuals. Communist influence also increased in the labor movement and in the electoral arena, but the American movement had no influence over international events. American Communists hailed FDR's "Quarantine the Aggressor" speech in October 1937, hoping it would lead to a collective security agreement or an end to the embargo blocking aid to the Spanish Loyalists. But their efforts toward these ends were unsuccessful. Instead, the Communist movement's political gains and its trend toward growth and stability came to an abrupt halt with the news of the signing of the Nazi-Soviet pact in August 1939.

While the movement declined, the musical trends of the Popular Front continued. The years 1939 to 1942 saw a folk music revival that contrasted sharply with the curtailment of experiments in literature, theater, and film. Two landmark musical events that took place within a few months of the signing of the Nazi-Soviet pact symbolized this revival. In the fall of 1939 Paul Robeson and the American People's Chorus performed "Ballad for Americans" in a CBS radio broadcast that reached millions of listeners. In March 1940 a "Grapes of Wrath" evening, a benefit for the John Steinbeck Committee, brought together traditional singers and popularizers who would continue to promote folk song as an important aspect of American culture. Will Geer played master of ceremonies in a program featuring Aunt Molly Jackson, Woody Guthrie, Leadbelly, Burl Ives, Pete Seeger, the Golden Gate Quartet, the American Square Dance Group, Alan Lomax, and Bess Lomax. The program included both traditional and folk-based topical songs, a mixture that would typify folk concerts and hootenannies for many years afterward.

Another sign of the folk song revival was the growing number of record companies and albums concerned with such music. Among the early recordings were Lawrence Gellert's *Negro Songs of Protest* and collections of Russian folk songs and American ballads. Keynote, which began production in 1940 with the famous Spanish Civil War album *Six Songs for Democracy*, published albums in the next few years by the Almanac Singers, Paul Robeson, Earl Robinson, and others. Some of the earliest recordings of Woody Guthrie, Pete Seeger, Leadbelly, Burl Ives, and other folk song revival artists were produced by Moses Asch, beginning in 1940. Over the years, the Asch, Disc, and later Folkways companies issued thousands of folk music albums.

In August 1940 CBS radio aired a half-hour pilot version of a folk music program called "Back Where I Come From," a project inspired by Alan Lomax. While the pilot was generally regarded as a success, no sponsor was willing to take on the show. CBS decided to continue the program anyway and signed Woody Guthrie on as a regular. This show was another way that the Left helped people appreciate folk material more. Earl Robinson says that people who heard Woody Guthrie, Richard Dyer-Bennett, Leadbelly, Pete Seeger, and the Golden Gate Quartet were made more aware of their heritage. According to Robinson, Alan Lomax chose socially conscious songs and stories, even though not explicitly "left stuff." For example, someone would sing "John Brown's Body," and Lomax would comment, "*There* was a war that was worth fighting."[2] In such ways were folk songs used to illustrate the CP line during the period of the Nazi-Soviet pact.

On a rainy day, February 10, 1940, FDR gave a speech to the American Youth Congress on the White House lawn. The AYC booed some of the president's remarks. For example, FDR spoke in favor of sending aid to Finland, a position which the AYC opposed, fearing this would lead the United States into war with the Soviet Union. Ironically, this event, which symbolized the end of the Communists' ties to their New Deal and Popular Front allies, was commemorated by a folk-style topical song written by Woody Guthrie: "Why Do You Stand There in the Rain?" The war years would be characterized by the creation of such folk-style songs and parodies, topical songs that extended the cultural concerns of the Popular Front era while illustrating the changing political outlook of the Communist movement. The difficulties inherent in blending a Popular Front approach to folk song as a weapon with the changing party line is clearly revealed in the career of the Almanac Singers.

Reporting on a Communist rally at Madison Square Garden in September 1939, James Wechsler claimed, "The thing that stood out in the meeting was the almost desperate huddling together of people confronted by a monumental world crisis, taking refuge in a reaffirmation of their own solidarity."[3] Communist cultural workers, and especially the Almanac Singers (formed in 1941), played a significant role in the reaffirmations of solidarity, community, and shared beliefs that helped hold the movement together during the Nazi-Soviet pact period. At a time when the movement was becoming isolated from many of its former allies and finding itself hard pressed to defend the sudden reversal of its antifascist policies, the Almanac songs unapologetically reinforced the Communist world view. The Almanacs' songs even affected some kids who were too young to understand the meaning and repercussions of the Nazi-Soviet pact. Ernie Lieberman was nine years old when the pact was declared. He says, "I knew something terrrible had happened, because the Jewish shopkeepers yelled at my mother." A few years later, Lieberman and others supported FDR and the war effort, their outlook changing in line with the Communist movement and the songs of the Almanac Singers.[4]

The original members of the Almanac Singers were Pete Seeger, Lee Hays, Millard Lampell, John Peter Hawes, and later

Woody Guthrie (who was on the West Coast when the group first formed in New York). By February 1941 the group was a functioning collective entity, writing and performing songs intended to provide topical commentary and reinforce the values of the Left. The Almanac Singers were aware of their novel position as the first urban folksinging group. Millard Lampell expressed the Almanacs' purpose in these terms: "We think this is the first time there has ever been an organized attempt . . . to sing the folksongs of America. We are trying to give back to the people the songs of the workers."[5] One significant aspect of the Almanacs' (and later People's Songs') outlook was the synonymous use of "the folk," "the people," and "the workers." Another aspect was expressed by Woody Guthrie: "The biggest parts of our song collection are aimed at restoring the right amount of people to the right amount of land and the right amount of houses and the right amount of groceries to the right amount of working folks."[6]

The Almanac Singers' use of song as a weapon, in other words, depended on the ideological view of the identity of folk songs with left-wing, progressive ideas. However, the Left occasionally acknowledged that not all folklore was inherently progressive. B. A. Botkin explained this in the foreword to *A Treasury of American Folklore:* "In one respect it is necessary to distinguish between folklore as we find it and folklore as we believe it ought to be. Folklore as we find it perpetuates human ignorance, perversity, and depravity along with human wisdom and goodness. Historically we cannot deny or condone this baser side of folklore—and yet we may understand and condemn it as we condemn other manifestations of human error."[7] The Almanac Singers frequently discussed songs and decided which ones they wanted to sing. While they sang traditional ballads and work songs, most of their songs consisted of new lyrics set to old folk tunes. This meant they did not have to confront the "ignorant, perverse, depraved," or conservative aspects of folklore.

The Almanac Singers' early creations were songs that illustrated their antiwar sentiments and the Communist movement's then-current line, "The Yanks Are Not Coming." Their first album was *Songs for John Doe*, recorded in March 1941. The album consisted of songs denouncing war and attacking Roosevelt's attempts at preparedness. One of the songs was "Plow Under":

> Remember when the AAA
> Killed a million hogs a day
> Instead of hogs it's men today—
> Plow the fourth one under.[8]

The most popular song was "The Ballad of October 16th," commemorating the initiation of the first peacetime draft in U.S. history. The chorus, set to the tune of "Jesse James," was a vicious attack on Roosevelt:

> Oh Franklin Roosevelt told the people how he felt
> We damned near believed what he said
> He said, "I hate war—and so does Eleanor,
> But we won't be safe till everybody's dead."[9]

After Germany attacked the Soviet Union on June 22, 1941, the CPUSA changed its antiwar position to one of support for the "people's war" against fascism, a move that many Communists greeted with relief and exhilaration. Lee Hays described how the shift to support for the president, preparedness, and war affected the Almanac Singers: "We were just about to leave for the West Coast when the war really started. Our whole politics took a terrible shift from 'the Yanks ain't coming' to 'the Yanks *are* coming.' All of a sudden it became one war, instead of two, and there was some chance of beating fascism on its own ground, which everybody was for. But it sure knocked hell out of our repertoire."[10]

The Almanacs' support of the war effort began with the writing and singing of "Reuben James," the story of the ninety-five people drowned in the first American ship torpedoed in World War II. In May 1942 they released an album called *Dear Mr. President,* calling for a reconciliation with FDR and the complete commitment of the United States to the war effort. The need for antifascist unity was expressed in such songs as "Deliver the Goods":

> The butcher, the baker, the tinker and the tailor
> Will all work behind the soldier and the sailor—

We're working in the cities, we're working in the woods
And we'll all work together to deliver the goods.[11]

The period following the Japanese attack on Pearl Harbor in December 1941 brought the Almanacs the promise of commercial success as their popularity began to extend beyond the Left. They were visited by a *Life* magazine photographer and received offers for an audition at the Rainbow Room (a fancy nightclub at the top of New York's Rockefeller Center), a record contract from Decca, and a management contract from the William Morris agency. The group performed for broadly sponsored war effort causes and programs, including network radio and Office of War Information (OWI) broadcasts. The Almanacs sang to nearly thirty million listeners at the opening of a new radio series, "This Is War," in February 1942. Three days later the group was attacked by the press for its recent peace repertoire and its Communist connections. The *New York World-Telegram* headline read "Singers on New Morale Show Also Warbled for Communists." The *New York Post* printed "'Peace' Choir Changes Tune." The Almanacs' offers from the popular music industry suddenly disappeared, and another wave of attacks by the press in January 1943 resulted in the end of their work with the OWI. The House Committee on Un-American Activities reported on the Almanac Singers in 1944, and in subsequent years right-wing organizations would repeatedly attack the group as Communist entertainers.[12]

Songs for John Doe reached a left-wing audience and perhaps some of the Communists' peculiar isolationist allies, such as the conservative America First Committee, during the Nazi-Soviet pact period. The Almanacs' prowar songs brought the group to the verge of commercial success. But the album that most closely expressed the Almanacs' world view and their view of how to use song as a weapon was *Talking Union*, recorded in late spring, 1941. The songs consisted of class-conscious lyrics, written by the Almanacs and others, set to traditional folk tunes. The Almanac Singers claimed the union hall was "the salvation of real honest-to-God American culture."[13] They expected their work with labor unions to be the primary means of "giving back to the people the songs of the workers." Their expectations were fueled by favorable receptions from workers, including nearly twenty thousand transport workers for whom they performed in Madison Square Garden in May 1941.

The singing, and therefore the influence, of *Talking Union* was cut short by the Communist movement's changes in policy. Following the attack on Pearl Harbor, the CPUSA began to support a no-strike pledge and other measures that called for employer-employee cooperation in the interests of the war effort. This suddenly made songs that emphasized class conflict inappropriate. Though unions made impressive numerical gains during the war, this was due more to maintenance-of-membership clauses than to militant action. The Almanac Singers maintained popularity among left-wing labor unions and radical groups and in fact began to reach a wider audience when they concentrated on cooperation in the war effort. Yet their shift in repertoire also undermined their success. The *Talking Union* songs remained more dear to the Left than those that called for union-management cooperation. After all, the former expressed the Communists' hopes and expectations of growing working-class consciousness in the long run. Woody Guthrie even wrote a satirical song about the problem of the shift in the party line causing a shift in the Almanacs' repertoire: "On Account of That *New* Situation."

> I started to sing a song
> To the entire population
> But I ain't a-doing a thing tonight
> On account of this new situation.[14]

The Almanac Singers were not responding to Comintern or CPUSA directives when they changed their repertoire to match a new political situation. Yet such a change illustrated the difficulty of being a cultural worker within the Communist movement and made the group vulnerable to the charge of being a "Communist front." According to Lee Hays, the Almanacs acted independently of the CPUSA. "When it came to shifts and turns in the Party line, I didn't pay any attention to them. I knew what I thought was right, and I wasn't gonna lose sleep over it. I'm sure Pete felt the same way. Woody would have said, 'The Almanacs—why that was just a bunch of old boys sitting around singing.'"[15] What Hays left out of this explanation is that "what I thought was right" was not a decision made in a vacuum, independent of other people and influences. The Almanac Singers were, of course, more than "just a bunch of old boys sitting around singing." They were part of a movement culture, which they helped to shape but which also defined their political outlook. The shared ideals and the dominant meanings and values of the movement culture provided the day-to-day impetus for their activity.

Their connection to the Communist movement inspired the Almanacs' work in many ways. It is therefore hardly surprising that the basic political tenets of that movement—such as the importance of the defense of the Soviet Union and the belief in the working class as the primary agent of change—affected the content of their songs. The Almanacs were skilled songwriters, and their songs were more than slogans. But their lyrics did not contradict the party line. Their independence was illustrated not by their political outlook so much as by their cultural theory—their commitment to the use of folk and topical songs as weapons.

The Almanacs' style and the substance of their pro-Roosevelt, antifascist songs attracted the media, the music industry, and the public. There is little question, then, that Red-baiting attacks emphasizing the source of the group's political outlook played a role in the Almanac Singers' dissolution. There were, however, other significant reasons for the group's decline. The war itself affected the group's dynamics, especially when Pete Seeger entered the army in July 1943. By this time, the size of the group in New York had become a problem. There were ten or twelve "members" of the Almanac Singers, making cooperative funding and booking arrangements difficult.

The group had musical and creative problems as well. While Woody Guthrie jokingly described the Almanac Singers as "the only group that rehearses on stage," he was seriously disturbed about the group's lack of attention to performance standards. He described his concern in a letter to his wife:

> I was trying to preach the idea that in a singing group . . . the ability to perform, play music or sing, had ought to be the first requirement, and that, within this singing group, if it was going to grow and spread and have a wide mass following, of course we would do everything in our power to make up songs and ballads that would spread the gospel of the working man, but that people who just naturally

could not sing, play an instrument, who never had before, and who it would take ten years to teach, I argued that our group should not be governed by the vote of such members, because, not understanding music, nor loving it enough to have already learned, although they may be very sympathetic and very anxious to . . . perform with us, the quality of the performances would not be good enough to win the long lasting respect of trade union audiences, much less white collar workers, or professional people, and much less the moneyed classes. To yank a girl out of the Bronx and shove a banjo in her hand and say, Come on and play and sing! That's funny, but it's not according to the facts.[16]

The optimism and enthusiasm of the Almanac Singers, as well as the problems they encountered, foreshadowed the efforts of People's Songs to use song as a weapon. The Red-baiting of the Almanacs was a prelude to attacks on People's Songsters and other left-wing artists during the cold war years. The relation of the two groups to the Communist movement was similar as well. The Almanac Singers were inspired by the Communist movement, which provided them with a world view and an audience. The movement enjoyed the entertainment and solidarity the singers provided, and the Almanacs' songs became a permanent part of the Communist movement culture. The Almanac Singers received favorable treatment in the movement press and at left-wing affairs. Yet the Communist leadership never offered the group any financial support. Pete Seeger says of the Almanacs: "We were orphans. There was no organization that really made themselves responsible for us."[17]

This meant that writers and performers constantly confronted the problem of making a living. If left-wing and union audiences could not or would not support them, they had to look elsewhere for an income. Yet they were strongly opposed to becoming tied to the demands of the popular music industry. They were convinced that they would never be able to sing the songs they wanted to sing and get paid for it. While popular Sunday afternoon folk concerts held in their loft helped pay the Almanacs' rent, the CPUSA leadership's indifference coupled with public anticommunism made it impossible for the group to survive in the long run.

Another problem was that radical folksingers in the 1940s at times ignored their own critical standards for judging songs and singers. The differing views of the Almanacs prompted some discussion of aesthetic questions. However, as Lee Hays explained their style, "The Almanacs had a way of doing their work first, and then if anyone wanted to construct a theory about it he was welcome to do so."[18] While the use of folk music and topical lyrics began to take precedence on the Left over the choral, art music–based tradition, political considerations often took priority in decisions about which songs should be sung and who should sing them. This is illustrated by the Almanacs dropping their best songs (their union songs) and by Woody Guthrie's complaints about the group's lack of performance standards.

The Almanacs faced the same basic problems that People's Songs would confront a few years later. There was a big difference between illustrating the party line in song and expressing the concerns of working people. The tension between expressing people's unarticulated needs and desires on the one hand and leading people to a more radical world view on the other was never resolved. The Almanacs did not often grapple with these problems on a theoretical level; they preferred to take direct action and learn from their experience. Yet they could not completely avoid such issues as their relationship with the bourgeois musical establishment, the need to make a living, their commitment to left-wing ideals, the lack of financial support from the Communist movement, and Red-baiting. The political and aesthetic questions about using folk song as a weapon were not resolved during the war years, when the American Communist outlook closely coincided with that of the American public. These problems confronted People's Songsters as they set out to continue the work of the Almanac Singers in the changed political context of the postwar period.

While the Almanac Singers had some success singing for labor unions—at rallies and strike meetings and on picket lines—they left a deeper impression on the Communist movement than they did on the labor movement. Pete Seeger, Lee Hays, and Woody Guthrie developed their ideas about folk song as a weapon while living, writing, and singing with the Almanacs. They also exposed some younger people to their ideas and their songs. The notion of song as a weapon, with an emphasis on the folk, the people, the workers, continued to develop during the war years. The use of a folk idiom for political purposes was kept alive by Woody Guthrie, for one. The inscription on his guitar, "This Machine Kills Fascists," encouraged Guthrie's admirers. For young leftists during the war years, "Woody remained an idol. We tried to play the guitar like he did and imitated the way he sang with Cisco Houston. We learned the Almanacs' *Talking Union* album by heart." Woody Guthrie and the Almanac Singers shaped some young people's view of the world, in particular their notion of "good guys and bad guys."[19]

The Almanacs also influenced people not yet committed to folk music and the Left. While stationed in San Francisco, Mario Casetta was introduced to folk music through Pete Seeger and the Almanac Singers. The music opened up a new world for Casetta, who had no political affiliation at that point. He claims that "the Almanacs and Pete Seeger started me in many ways." Casetta ran out and bought records, having been convinced that music could be used effectively for political action. "Not only was this stuff good, but here is the way to do it. Here is something for the good guys. . . . And from that moment I became involved."[20] Casetta's first involvement was through the California Labor School, with which he did singing, street performing, and political action, mostly aimed at getting FDR reelected. Casetta also talked with Pete Seeger on Saipan about starting People's Songs, and he was totally involved with the Los Angeles chapter from its inception.

David Sear became interested in folk music at the Little Red Schoolhouse, where he heard the Almanac Singers and Leadbelly. Sear says he got "turned on" hearing "Old Joe Clark," which during the war became "Round and Round Hitler's Grave." "I really loved the sound of the driving southern mountain music . . . and the relevancy of the words," says Sear. "That music really grabbed me, and the connection of what people were doing with it."[21] Sear further developed his interest in folk music in the American Folksay group, at Camp Woodland, and at Camp Wo-Chi-Ca, settings in which he sang and played the banjo.

The American Folksay group in New York City was one of the major institutions in which young people simultaneously learned songs and developed their political outlook. Folksay began as a dance group in 1942, entertaining at war-relief rallies, USO benefits, and similar affairs. It became a group committed to promoting the American democratic heritage by joining American folk dance and music with left-wing politics. Its slogan during the war was "Folk Culture—A Weapon for Victory." By 1944 it had affiliated with American Youth for Democracy, becoming the only AYD branch that had to limit new memberships because of its size. It performed at many functions connected with the war effort, while its evenings of folk dancing, singing, and socializing became a focal point for many young leftists. Membership ranged from fourteen- to eighteen-year-olds, but an exception was made for Ernie Lieberman, who at thirteen was the youngest member of the group. He describes what the American Folksay group meant to him: "The central activity was to provide a Saturday evening of square and folk dancing with an 'intermission show' every two weeks at the Furriers Union Hall on 26th Street. I was just learning to play the guitar and it was a wonderful opportunity for me to perform in the shows for a young audience of two hundred or more on a regular basis. We also started to take these shows on the road for other organizations in and around the city."[22]

The other major institution that brought together folk songs and left-wing politics were the New York summer camps. Along with American Folksay, Camp Wo-Chi-Ca made a big impression on Irwin Silber, David Sear, Ernie Lieberman, Ronnie Gilbert, and Jerry Silverman, among others. For example, Jerry Silverman says his interest in music was shaped by his experiences at Camp Wo-Chi-Ca, where he first heard the recordings of Woody Guthrie's dust bowl ballads and the songs of the Lincoln Brigade and learned to play the guitar. Ronnie Gilbert says that at Camp Wo-Chi-Ca her social and political life merged, a blend that continued for many years. Another former camper describes the role of music at Wo-Chi-Ca in the summer of 1942:

> When I got there that summer singing had already become an integral part of every activity in the camp. Naomi Feld, a young, enthusiastic choral conductor had turned the camp into a singing camp. The vehicle was the chorus, which became an overflow activity in its own right and through its members infected the camp with the songs they learned there. We sang everywhere: while cleaning up the bunk (you could do a whole "Ballad For Americans"), walking from one activity

> to another, at meals, campfires and any formal gatherings. . . . Naomi's enthusiasm . . . was contagious. We learned to sing with great verve and deep feeling for the material. 'Singing is a form of battle' was a slogan she introduced to us.[23]

Records had to provide the continuity between one summer and the next, until Wo-Chi-Ca started a winter program that included a chorus. The chorus sang the same songs but for a wider audience. Being interracial and nondenominational, it was accepted in a variety of settings, from churches in Harlem to Russian War Relief to the New York Fresh Air Fund.

Fred Hellerman says that he was attracted to the Left in his early high school days. He joined the YCL, met Ronnie Gilbert at Wo-Chi-Ca, and, through the Almanacs and Woody and Leadbelly, discovered a body of music that dealt with subjects other than love. He began playing guitar while in the service during World War II and after the war met more people with similar interests and began to sing more actively.[24]

Pete Seeger's view of song as a weapon was also shaped decisively during this period. Seeger traveled with Woody Guthrie during the summer of 1940, returning to New York with an "astonishing feeling of independence. I realized I'd never starve to death as long as I had a voice and a banjo." After singing with Woody Guthrie in labor unions and with Lee Hays at fund-raising parties and other left-wing affairs in New York City, Seeger became convinced that "there was a job we could do, intellectually and organizationally. We could make a singing labor movement, take up where Joe Hill left off, and carry the tradition on." Seeger thought that "Woody's and Lee's method of writing songs made sense, taking old tunes and putting new words to them, not getting picky about being original all the time."[25]

The war may have disrupted the Almanac Singers, but it gave folk music a new audience. Pete Seeger found his singing appreciated by the enlisted men on Saipan. Other cultural workers who would become active in People's Songs also used music to support the war effort. These included G.I. Felix Landau and USO singer Betty Sanders.

Those who did not join the armed forces supported the war effort at home. Ronnie Gilbert went to Washington, D.C., where she met Jackie Gibson and joined the Priority Ramblers. The group's "priorities" were folk and country songs about the war effort and other social issues.[26]

Waldemar Hille began to write prowar, pro-Roosevelt songs while he was choral director at Elmhurst College in Illinois. He brought back left-wing songs from New York, including Lawrence Gellert's *Negro Songs of Protest* and Russian songs. While the songs interested the students, they worried the school authorities. Hille left Elmhurst and went to Highlander, where he both learned and composed more left-wing songs. At the end of the war, he worked with Lee Hays in New York, carrying on his "progressive musical activity" as music director of War Prisoners Aid.[27]

Communist cultural workers, among others, came out of World War II with a profound, yet misunderstood, sense of unity with the American people. The Communist movement paid little attention to the fact that its relative prestige and influence was due not only to its own efforts but to the temporary muting of anticommunist and anti-Soviet sentiments during the Popular Front and the years of U.S.-Soviet alliance during the war. Young artists such as Pete Seeger shared an uncritical commitment to the movement and to vague communist ideals; at the same time, they particularly identified with the political ideals and tactics of the Popular Front and war years. Those who would found People's Songs shared strong sentiments about the importance of democracy, unity with the American people, internationalism, and the power of song as a weapon. These ideas were not the result of CP leaders' cynical manipulation of rank-and-file Communists; they were neither articulated systematically nor conceived of as a theory of social change. Rather, they were a series of inchoate feelings based on a unique blend of ideology and experience.

If the Teheran conference symbolized cooperation between the capitalist and communist worlds, the change from the CPUSA to the Communist Political Association (CPA) in 1944 symbolized Browder's final Americanizing touch, intended to enhance domestic unity and acceptance of Communists. The preamble to the CPA constitution described it as a "non-party organization of Americans which, basing itself upon the working class, carries forward the traditions of Washington, Jefferson, Paine, Jackson, and Lincoln, under the changed conditions of modern industrial society."[28]

Though Browder's promotion of the CPA and the Teheran line would lead to his downfall after World War II, in the short run both ideas were popular. The recruiting drive that followed these changes brought the Communist movement back to the level of strength it had attained in 1938–39. Browder found support for his long-range policy that, "while remaining essentially faithful to Russian interests, would place heavy stress upon absorbing the CP into the ordinary political life of the country: a postwar Popular Front extending into the indefinite future."[29]

Given their sentiments and activities, and the Communist movement's strength and optimism at the end of the war, it was no wonder People's Songsters had high hopes for the postwar fate of song as a weapon. Yet for all the excitement about Americanism, democracy, and international cooperation, the Communist movement was more the same than different in these critical areas. Young cultural workers had survived the movement's political crises, such as the Moscow trials and the Nazi-Soviet pact, like other Communists, with their faith intact. For example, after the Moscow trials Pete Seeger was convinced that Stalin was a "pretty tough customer." Yet he rationalized his belief that the CP was telling the truth about the purge trials being genuine confessions by assuring himself that you needed tough, direct-action type people to make a revolution.[30] Young Communists continued to accept changes in the party line because they believed that the people at the top making decisions were the ones who cared the most and were the most knowledgeable and informed. Perhaps more important, though, was the fact that that young cultural workers had discovered a new, exciting musical form with which to try and change the world.

Praise for folk music and its politics appeared in the movement press during the war years, as in the *People's World* story of May 1941: "Paul Robeson Says: There's Solidarity in People's Song."[31] When cultural critic Samuel Sillen called for high-quality war songs in a May 1942 *New Masses* article, he was answered by partisans who emphasized the value of American folk songs for the war effort. Earl Robinson wrote that Sillen was looking for songs in the wrong place: "In looking for a people's song in a people's war, he should have looked not only among the completely commercial manifestations of Tin Pan Alley, but among the people themselves, the trade unions and progressive organizations. If he had, he would have seen signs of this rising new people's culture. . . . A very significant thing about these songs . . . is the fact that they are almost entirely based on tried and true Americana, the old folk songs our common people have been singing ever since they arrived here."[32] Millard Lampell wrote that the songs to compare with "John Brown's Body" were still being written: "What makes good songs? I think that the answer is in folk music. The Spanish loyalists sang folk songs. The Red Army is singing folk songs and so are the Chinese. Folk songs, songs in the people's language and in the people's tradition. Songs made up yesterday and this morning."[33]

But the favorable press reflected the commitment of composers and performers rather than the movement leadership's appreciation for people's songs. During the war years the political use of folk music, and cultural matters in general, were not a high priority among Communist leaders, who became more and more preoccupied with what they viewed as more pressing ideological matters. Yet a light-hearted story told by Ben Dobbs indicates the continued importance of singing as a form of international communication among rank-and-file Communists. Dobbs, a platoon sergeant in the U.S. Army during World War II, was in Czechoslovakia just after it was liberated in April 1945. He told his captain he was going to look for the Communist party in Pilsen. (It was no secret that Dobbs was an organizer for the CPUSA.) As Dobbs tells it,

> I found a place where there were obviously Communist sympathizers. . . . They directed me to . . . a room full of young people . . . and I came in there and told them I was looking for some Communists that I could sympathize with, told them I was an American Communist. And a hush fell over the room. There were about fifty people there. I was in full battle array. . . . And they looked at me and they said, "Do you know any songs?" And for the life of me I couldn't think of a song. So I sang a song that we used to sing in the YCL—it was called the Red Air Fleet song. And they were not familiar with it. . . . They all gathered around and brought out balalaikas and guitars, and then *they* sang a song. And I couldn't think of another song, so I

sang . . . "Casey Jones" . . . the IWW version of it [Casey Jones, the engineer turned scab]. . . . That was unfamiliar. Then *they* sang a song. And then it dawned on me what they wanted. . . . What they wanted me to sing was the "Internationale." So when I sang that, then all the kissing and hugging took place, and I was accepted into the group, and then they brought me to the headquarters of the Communist party of Pilsen.[34]

It was not, however, such rank-and-file solidarity that guided the international Communist movement. While American left-wing cultural workers promoted a broad, democratic Popular Front spirit through folk song, the leaders of international Communism began to point a new direction for the movement. As People's Songs set out to "create and promote songs of labor and the American people," the American Communist movement changed its line in response to the cold war.

4

"My Song Is My Weapon": People's Songs, the CPUSA, and the Cold War

FDR's death in April 1945 was mourned by millions of Americans, including many Communists who wept as openly as anyone. Though they could not have known it at the time, Truman's succession would lead shortly to the obsession with Communism and disloyalty that defined the domestic cold war. As the United States and the Soviet Union moved to consolidate their positions, the Truman administration helped generate an atmosphere of crisis. The shift to a permanent war economy, supported by the doctrines of cold war and national security, meant that the American public had to give tacit consent to preparation for a limitless range of military threats. *Fortune* summed up the changed outlook: "The only way to avoid having American policy dominated by crisis is to live in crisis—prepared for war."[1]

At the same time, the Communist movement shifted to a more orthodox, sectarian outlook, predicting economic crisis and growing class consciousness. The United States was attacked as the center of reaction and imperialism; the threat of American fascism and World War III, argued the Communists, could only be countered by a vigorous offensive. The implications of cold war anticommunism and the Communist movement's renewed orthodoxy were not apparent to the approximately thirty folksingers, chorus directors, union education officials, and others who met in Pete Seeger's Greenwich Village basement December 31, 1945, to found People's Songs. In Pete Seeger's words: "In 1945 Americans came home from the war. We dived enthusiastically into long deferred projects."[2] The enthusiasm, optimism, and naiveté with which Seeger and others did "dive in" to People's Songs characterized the organization throughout its existence. Their broad aims and perspective are indicated best in the following excerpt from a People's Songs recruiting document:

What Is People's Songs?

People all over the world and all over this country have always been making up songs about the things that were on their minds. Work songs, play songs, nonsense songs, religious songs and fighting songs. Put them all together—that's what we call "People's Songs." There's only one thing wrong—or maybe right—with them—they're not commercial. They don't have love-dove, June-croon in them, they're not slick enough and they talk about life as it really is.

Now then, in December of 1945 a bunch of people who'd learned to love and know these songs and the people from whom they come, who'd done their share of adding to them and singing them around, singers and songwriters like Pete Seeger and Lee Hays, like Woody Guthrie and Josh White, like Bess Hawes and Millard Lampell and Earl Robinson got together one evening and decided to do something about it. So, on $150 collected from among themselves in chunks of 5 and 10 dollars, they started this organization they called People's Songs, Inc. to spread these songs around, to bring to as many people as possible, the true democratic message that came out of this music.[3]

Those who attended the founding meeting of People's Songs did contribute money, which was used to rent a small office on West 42nd Street in New York City. The space was shared with Stage for Action, a radical drama group with similar aims. The group began publication of the monthly *People's Songs Bulletin*, available through membership subscriptions, and set up a separate booking agency called People's Artists to handle the arrangement of performances by People's Songs musicians. Money for these and other activities came from hootenannies, booking fees, subscriptions and advertising money brought in by the *Bulletin*, and later from sales of *The People's Song Book*.

In addition to those mentioned above, Jackie Gibson, Ronnie Gilbert, Irwin Silber, and David Sear were among those involved with the New York chapter of People's Songs from the beginning. Pete Seeger served as director, and after a few months Waldemar Hille was asked to be music editor of the *Bulletin;* in 1947 Irwin Silber was asked to run the business and organizational end of things. Mario Casetta had talked with Pete Seeger on Saipan, when the latter envisioned creating "a loosely-knit organization, some structure where people could get together to exchange and print songs."[4] As a result of Seeger's encouragement and some discussion with Earl Robinson, Casetta started the Los Angeles branch of People's Songs, with which he was thoroughly involved for the next three years. As Casetta says, Los Angeles was *the* place for People's Songs outside of New York, boasting a strong organization that hosted crowded meetings, workshops, and hootenannies. Money from the latter kept the office going and paid Casetta's salary as executive secretary. Under his direction, the People's Songs office provided performers for picket lines, demonstrations, and fund-raising parties, usually for little or no pay.

People's Songs carried on a multitude of activities during its three-year life span. The national office in New York led the way by collecting songs and keeping a library; producing the monthly *Bulletin* and song books, song sheets, filmstrips, and records; and organizing concerts, hootenannies, and local engagement tours for various performers. New York activists also taught classes on such subjects as music for political action. Other activities suggested by the national office included fostering the formation of new local performing groups, establishing a songwriters committee to encourage local amateur songwriters to make up songs reflecting their own experiences and problems, and creating local People's Songs radio programs.

The New York chapter tended to favor folk songs, but from its inception People's Songs contained non-folk-song-oriented musicians with jazz and popular music interests, as well as those from the workers' chorus and classical traditions. In theory, at least, the organization was highly tolerant of varied forms of music. Pop writers such as Harold Rome, Morris Goodson and Sonny Vale, and E. Y. "Yip" Harburg wrote "people's songs." The Los Angeles branch, in particular, demonstrated People's Songs' musical diversity, containing folk enthusiasts, Hollywood artists, and popular songwriters and performers. Mario Casetta says there was no elitism. "Anything was grist for our mill if it would work."[5]

People's Songs' initial efforts were very successful. The organization attracted a thousand members within a year and formed chapters in the United States and Canada. It also established encouraging contacts with unions. People's Songs members sang on the picket lines of striking Westinghouse workers in Pittsburgh, recorded an album of election songs for the CIO's political action committee, and produced a filmstrip for the National Maritime Union. They also performed at rallies to save the Office of Price Administration (which was being dismantled by Congress) and joined the California housing caravan which traveled to Sacramento to demand better housing legislation.

People's Songs initially received positive responses from the mainstream press. The *New York Times* greeted the new organization favorably, explaining that "People's Songs keeps a musical stethoscope on the heartbeat of the nation, translating current events into notes and lyrics."[6] *Fortune* magazine promoted the idea of song as a weapon: "Americans love a party even on the picket line, and union organizers are well aware that there is strength in fun. A racy song helps strikers over some tense hours, and if the tune is catching it may do more to persuade the public than an armful of press releases."[7] An editorial in the *Christian Science Monitor* welcomed the new receptive audience for American folk songs: "It is interesting to speculate on the possible role of People's Songs groups in their communities. They can certainly do much to circulate the still all-too-neglected folk heritage of poetry and song which, as Archibald MacLeish has said, 'tells more about the American people than all the miles of their quadruple-lane express highways and all the acres of their billboard-plastered cities.'"[8]

The purposeful blending of democracy, music, and politics was emphasized in People's Songs internal documents. While its written documents probably did not define how People's Songs actually functioned in various cities, these documents do reveal the general tone, approach, and goals of the organization. For example, "Organize a People's Songs Branch" suggested that the first meeting of a People's Songs chapter should include a description of "these jobs that People's Songs can do":

a. Teach everyone some grand new songs
b. Get memberships to singing
c. Get kids singing

d. Songs as a political weapon, an organizing weapon
e. Get new songs made up
f. Throughout emphasize the value of music for brotherhood and peace[9]

It was suggested that those who called a first meeting invite educational directors of local unions; local progressive organizations such as American Youth for Democracy, Progressive Citizens of America, and the International Workers Order; music teachers; and progressive and cultural leaders of the community—the people who might be interested in joining a People's Songs chapter. However, the ultimate goal was for these songs to reach a broad spectrum of "the people." The Preamble to People's Songs International Constitution expresses the group's vision:

> We believe that the songs of any people truly express their lives, their struggles and their highest aspirations. Just as the old songs—whether they be ballads, love songs, lullabies, dance tunes, or broadsides of the events of the day—played a role in the past, songs today must tell the story of the present. We further believe that songs and other cultural forms must be used to enrich the lives of common people everywhere and to this end we dedicate ourselves to the dissemination of all people's songs to new and broader audiences. And we extend a welcoming hand to anyone, no matter what religion or creed or race or nation, who believes with us that songs must bring about a stronger unity between all people to fight for peace, for a better life for all, and for the brotherhood of man.[10]

What did People's Songsters mean by "the people?" The term suggests both how vague and how ambitious was People's Songs' program, for "the people" included almost everyone. The more political Communists insisted that "the people" meant the working class and its allies; they continued to expect that the working class would play a leading role in bringing about revolutionary social change. The more cultural Communists did not express a notion of class as part of their definition of "the people." It was a broad, populist concept, as expressed in Carl Sandburg's *The People, Yes*. "The people" meant "all the people," excluding only big capitalists and racists—anyone whom People's Songs might hope to reach with its broad progressive message.[11]

People's Songs' broad outlook and folksy language indicate the group's roots in the Popular Front, its distance from postwar political and cultural trends, and its naive faith in the power of song. Though People's Songsters' cultural theory was never well defined, their approach was based on a sincere belief that the popularization of people's songs would "help people live better lives."[12] Irwin Silber described People's Songs' outlook in the 1961 publication, *Reprints from the People's Songs Bulletin:* "We thought that the world was worth saving and that we could do it with songs."[13] This could be done in a variety of ways, according to the participants. Pete Seeger's vision was creating "a singing labor movement," while David Sear thought a central purpose of People's Songs was "popularizing and making known our American folk music."[14]

Fred Hellerman says, "The stated purpose was to change the world. . . . Another purpose, a good purpose, was becoming a central point for people with like interests and goals to establish contact." People's Songs thus served as "a rallying point," a way for people to exchange and build songs and experience and to grow together. In a similar vein, Waldemar Hille stated People's Songs' purposes as giving a cultural voice, in an organized way, to people's progressive feelings and making material and performers available for rallies and picket lines. In the short run, then, People's Songs encouraged the creation of new songs and served as a point of exchange for those who wanted to share songs for use, thereby making material and performers available for progressive causes. As one subscriber recalled, People's Songs "served a direct purpose for me, gave me songs to sing. . . . I wasn't looking for the grand design, just wanted songs to learn," for use in teaching and performing.[15]

People's Songs thus functioned as a forum for communication among progressive songwriters and performers in particular. Still, the group's ambitions went far beyond this immediate purpose. People's Songs assumed that popularizing folk and topical songs would return the folk heritage to people, educate people about important issues, and encourage creativity and activism. People's Songsters' optimism was based in part on their faith in the creativity of human beings and their desire to express the yearnings of the people for a better world. Woody

Guthrie expressed this in his own way: "Let me be known as the man who told you something you already know."[16]

Underlying this view of their work was People's Songsters' identification of folk music with left-wing politics. They believed that popularizing the songs would spread the political message as well. This point was expressed in one performer's later explanation of the purpose of People's Songs, which, he said, was "reaching the masses of America with our political message through the vehicle of folk songs, which were their music, only they didn't know it. As they found out about it, they would think it was wonderful, and they would take it up, not through the mass media . . . but through the streets and through small meeting halls and get-togethers and hootenannies, and whatever. So it was a means of spreading the message *and* the songs, which were bound inextricably together."[17] But spreading the message and the songs became increasingly difficult as the cold war intensified and the Communist movement's influence and popularity declined.

At the end of World War II the CPUSA was relatively strong, having helped FDR's reelection campaign in 1944, maintained control in a number of CIO unions, and increased its ranks (even after the CPUSA dissolved to become the CPA in 1944). Certain postwar conditions appeared to favor the movement's continued growth and influence: a strike wave, indications of support for an independent political party based on the labor movement, and the strength of organizations which the Communists had helped form and in which they were still accepted (National Negro Congress, American Youth for Democracy, National Lawyers' Guild). Yet American Communism shortly began to decline and experience a crisis from which it never recovered. The Communists' misguided postwar "offensive," coupled with their "defensive" reactions to government attacks and the fear of fascism (which included internal purges and sending leaders underground), led only to self-destruction.

The Communists' return to orthodoxy after World War II was manifest in the party's reconstitution, William Z. Foster's replacement of Earl Browder as its leader, and the hardening of positions on a variety of issues, including culture. Maurice Isserman describes the critical difference between Browder's and Foster's leadership:

> "Browderism" held the potential for leading to something other than itself—sheltering and lending legitimacy to the efforts of those American Communists who had the capacity for and commitment to finding what would later be described as the "American Road to Socialism"—even if in 1944 and 1945 taking any road to socialism was the last thing on Browder's mind. Foster looked to political and economic cataclysms—a new depression, the triumph of fascism in America, a third world war—as the motor for social change. It was all right for the Communists to dabble in coalition politics in the meantime, as they would with the Progressive party campaign in 1948, but that could never represent more than a tactical orientation. When it came time to launch the struggle for socialism, when events had finally produced a working class ready to respond to revolutionary leadership, the Communists would follow the classic outline derived from the Bolsheviks' experience in 1917.[18]

Another problem the movement confronted was that the war years had brought about a further widening of the split between the world of the CP leadership and the rank and file. As new members were recruited during the war, the party returned to the more loosely structured, neighborhood-based organizing model which had been abandoned during the Nazi-Soviet pact. From that point on, according to Isserman, "Some Communists would be encouraged to think of the party as a kind of left-wing Kiwanis Club, while others would continue to be judged and judge themselves by that 'yardstick of the professional revolutionist.'"[19] This split was as evident in the cultural realm as anywhere else, where the narrow concept of art as a weapon was revived with a vengeance.

The narrow interpretation of "art as a weapon" always surfaced in periods when the CP claimed to be on the offensive in the struggle for revolutionary socialism. It had been dominant during the Third Period, inspiring the creation of proletarian art, and it became visible again at the end of World War II when the party took the offensive against what it saw as American fascism and imperialism.

People's Songsters shared significant aspects of the CP's narrow approach to cultural work, expecting songs with the correct viewpoint to have an immediate political impact on people. This expectation was described by one People's Songster: "We thought that songs were a weapon in the sense that they could change people and . . . inspire people to great deeds and that they could bring everybody over to our way of thinking."[20] Another People's Songster declared that he didn't like to be called a progressive entertainer: "I feel that the kind of work I, and other People's Songs members are doing is a direct organizing job."[21] Yet People's Songs' activity did not reflect the CP's return to orthodoxy. People's Songsters did not follow the party line on how to use art as a weapon. By and large they were unaware of the Communist movement's internal debates and policy statements on cultural matters.

The gap between People's Songs and the CPUSA is illustrated by an event that convulsed party cultural circles in 1946. In February of that year, novelist and screenwriter Albert Maltz published an article in *New Masses* entitled "What Shall We Ask of Writers?" Maltz criticized the literary Left for vulgarizing the slogan "art as a weapon" by emphasizing the weapon of formal ideology and neglecting the nature of art. Such judgments, argued Maltz, led to absurdities "such as the *New Masses* critic attacking Lillian Hellman's 'Watch on the Rhine' when it was produced as a play in 1940, because its anti-Nazi politics were anathema during the period of the Stalin-Hitler pact, and then hailing it as a film in 1942 after Hitler's invasion of Russia."[22] Maltz's article was fiercely attacked in the Communist press by cultural critics and writers who criticized its viewpoint for being anti-Marxist. In the pages of the *New Masses*, for example, Howard Fast, Joseph North, Alvah Bessie, John Howard Lawson, and others argued in essence that politics had to come first in creating and evaluating a work of art.[23] Maltz was denounced in party circles and soon after published a second article retracting the first.[24] In April 1946 the *New Masses* and *Daily Worker* sponsored a symposium on "Art as a Weapon." Within a week of this event, William Z. Foster published an article in *New Masses* entitled "Elements of a People's Cultural Policy." Foster began by stating that art is a weapon in class struggle and pointing out that the main danger in the cultural field is the "Right danger." Foster maintained that the party cultivated artistic freedom while insisting on theoretical clarity. He concluded that the "necessary rectifications" in the party's understanding and practice were being made, as the course of the Maltz debate made clear. Many Communists took this to be the final word on the subject.[25]

The "Maltz incident" is often cited by scholars to indicate the narrow and dogmatic direction of Communist cultural work in the postwar period.[26] Yet this incident had no direct effect on People's Songs. Most People's Songsters were unaware of Maltz's article and the ensuing controversy. They did not participate in the debate, did not follow the party intellectuals' dogmatic stand about how to measure the quality of a work of art, did not narrow their range of songs, and did not abandon their broad, populist approach to cultural work.

People's Songsters were also unaware of major statements of cultural policy on the part of Comintern and CPUSA cultural commissars. For example, at a conference called by the Central Committee of the Soviet CP in 1947, Andrei Zhdanov delivered a speech to Soviet musicians in which he attacked formalism and the decadence of modern bourgeois music. The postwar years are often referred to as the "Zhdanov era," symbolizing the emphasis on ideological conformity. Zhdanov's American counterpart was V. J. Jerome, who made a 1947 speech called "Culture in a Changing World, A Marxist Approach." Jerome acknowledged the importance of aesthetics, stating that "for art to be a weapon, it must first be art." He praised independent cultural activities, including the work of People's Songs. Yet Jerome also expressed the CPUSA's mechanistic, sectarian outlook, attacking pragmatism, existentialism, idealism, nihilism (and the art inspired by such "isms"), praising the Soviet Union as the staunchest defender of cultural democracy, and quoting with approval Stalin's characterization of artists as "engineers of the soul."[27] Such statements revealed, among other things, Communist conservatism in the cultural realm, characterized by a focus on high art and condemnation of literary and musical experiments. Like the Maltz controversy and Foster's statement on cultural policy, however, speeches such as Zhdanov's and Jerome's did not define People's Songs' cultural theory or guide the organization in its work.

People's Songsters did look to the CPUSA for *political* guidance, and they performed at a variety of party functions. However, even though many People's Songs officials were also party members, the organization itself had no formal ties with the CPUSA and it did not look to the party for *cultural* guidance. Waldemar Hille says he knew the CP had a cultural commission, but he was unsure of what they did. There was a party folk music club, one of several subdivisions of the music section of the CP, but this club did not directly plan the policies of People's Songs. Nor did the party contribute money to People's Songs—a sign that the leadership did not view People's Songs' work as essential.

The CP never paid as much attention to folksinging as it did to other forms of art and music. For example, the cultural journal *New Masses* regularly discussed literature, theater, film, and classical music, while folksingers appeared almost exclusively in advertisements for particular events. A few isolated articles appeared in the *Daily Worker* and *New Masses,* but the only regular coverage of People's Songs' activities was a column in *People's World* written by "Boots" Casetta. Waldemar Hille thought that he and Pete Seeger were seen as being off-base with their broad, American approach to culture.[28]

The CPUSA never shared People's Songs' belief in the potential of song as a weapon to reach out to the people. Folksingers were seen as useful within the movement as left-wing entertainers; they could provide a break in a meeting or rally, or perform at the end after the serious business had been concluded. In other words, their role was to entertain and encourage those already committed to the movement. In this regard, despite the increasing popularity of folk songs since the 1930s, the CP's attitude in the 1940s had not changed much. This attitude is illustrated by George Charney's dismayed reaction to a 1936 speech given by a national CP representative at the New England district convention: "He made a two-hour speech and we hung on every word expecting a brilliant analysis of world affairs; but most of his speech dealt with the importance of mass singing. A people who can sing will make a revolution; a people without spontaneous song will never defy the gods. And this went on for two hours. I always liked 'Bandiera Rossa,' but this was really stretching a point. A hootenanny revolutionist!"[29]

People's Songsters were unable to convince party leaders of the serious potential power of song. Singer-songwriter Malvina Reynolds quit the party because the leadership "had no concept of what I was doing or of what effect it would have."[30] Mario Casetta claims that with the proper use of songs meetings could have given people an aesthetic lift so that they would come out charged up and feeling good; instead, people had to sit through long speeches. The talent of people's artists as entertainers was valued within party circles, yet even in this context folksingers often felt they were treated with a lack of respect. Jerry Silverman describes being the obligatory folksinger at a meeting, waiting and waiting to go on and finally appearing while the coffee and cake were being served. Other performers echo this feeling that the party did not pay enough attention to folksingers and underestimated the importance of songs.[31]

Contrary to the myth of heavy-handedness, the CP for the most part left the folk song movement, especially People's Songs, to its own devices. This may have been simply a result of the party's high art and mass culture preferences, which contrasted with the commitment to folk song and the anticommercial feeling of People's Songsters. Participants speculate that perhaps the party thought that People's Songs was doing well on its own, or that cultural workers could not be controlled anyway, or that they just weren't important enough to command attention. There is probably a grain of truth in each of these explanations. More than anything else, it seems that the party took the work of People's Songsters for granted, enjoying their function as entertainers as an adjunct to important political tasks.

The party's attitude was symbolized by the fight performers were forced to wage in order to get paid for their work. While it became standard to have a folksinger at a meeting, the expectation was that a performer would donate his or her services. This assumption created bitter feelings on the part of some performers. As one explained, the party was used to paying the cost of printing written material, renting a hall, and serving refreshments, yet the singers were supposed to come free. "We had to fight a continuing battle to be paid for our work," says Earl Robinson. Not only was it difficult for performers to make a living and to feel that their work was respected, but the irony of the Left's exploitation of cultural workers was not lost on the singers. They continue, even today, to repeat this story: When a woman asked Woody Guthrie to sing free of charge "for a good cause," his response was, "Lady, I don't sing for bad causes."[32]

Although People's Songs and the CPUSA had some differences, in general the interaction between the two organizations benefited both individual musicians and the movement as a whole. With hindsight, many People's Songsters agree that the short-term effects of song as a weapon were felt chiefly within the movement. Songs were an important means of providing emotional support, encouraging people by offering a sense of togetherness and unity. The feelings of former People's Songsters are corroborated by those within the movement who claim that they and others were affected by songs. The more strictly political activists may not have shared the depth of People's Songsters' faith in the power of song; still, they agree that "song is a marvelous weapon." Dorothy Healey, an organizer who believed that art as a weapon moved people, broadened their horizons, and gave them a sense of identity, states: "For me . . . the most important aspect of art as a weapon was in the singing. It was the songs that united people, that gave them a sense of identity."[33] Ben Dobbs, another activist who viewed songs as an important means of unifying the movement, echoes People's Songs' claim that songs were superior to speeches. Dobbs found it impossible to speak after someone sang a song because "you can't say it better than that."[34]

Songs played an important supportive role for the party and the movement. In turn, the movement provided a supportive audience for people's artists, serving as a musical training ground for writers and performers. As one People's Songs performer expressed it: "I grew up in a unique set of circumstances provided by the Communist-led left in that historical moment that paralleled my growing up on the streets and in the schools of Brooklyn. The left provided me with caring adults, friends, a culture, an ideology, a community. It taught me a vocation, gave me the opportunity to practice it and peers to learn from."[35]

The Communist movement attracted, cultivated, and provided an audience for many talented writers and performers. These artists contributed to the movement's impact, supporting its activities and, in the long run, broadening its outreach. This was not in the 1930s when artists in general moved to the left, treating social themes and focusing on the lives of working-class people. The crisis of the postwar period was expressed very differently in cultural terms than were reactions to the problems of the 1930s. There was a distinct shift away from the social consciousness of the 1930s as artists "lost faith in the possibility of resolving public issues and . . . rejected society." Alienation became the major theme in the arts. Literature and art were regarded as autonomous, with the art object "having its being only in an aesthetic context and in isolation from society." In literature, naturalism gave way to modernism; in painting, the turn toward abstract expressionism, as in the work of Jackson Pollock, has been described as "a rejection of culture and history."[36] Critics complained that mass culture reinforced passivity and tried to cage the unconscious and that the media was controlled by a "tribe of intermediary bureaucrats."[37] Yet the cultural crisis was not met by a concerted effort on the Left to provide an alternative. Socially conscious graphic art, documentary expression, and experiments in literature, theater, and film were not rejuvenated. There was no support from the government for such efforts. Left-wing artists who had worked their way into the mass media were about to be attacked, beginning with the Hollywood Ten. The Left was narrowing its political and cultural outlook, with culture receiving less sustained attention as the anti-Communist attacks began. There was no gifted, committed younger generation coming of age—except in the world of folk music. People's Songsters' creation and performance of folk and topical songs sustained a vanishing concept of social consciousness in the arts while providing a broader approach to art as a weapon than that demanded by the Communist cultural elite. Because of their anomalous position, in American society and on the Left, they provided a clear test of the direct effects of song as a weapon.

How was song as a weapon supposed to work? People's Songs saw its work as the continuation of a tradition that included the Hutchinson family (abolitionist singers), nineteenth-century labor balladeers, the IWW, early socialist singers, and others.[38] Like these predecessors, People's Songs would use songs to protest, to educate, to build solidarity and morale. People's Songs added to this tradition a focus on folk-style songs—the music of the people themselves—and encouraged people to create their own songs.

The most common method of promoting song as a weapon

was to emphasize that a song had a different appeal than a speech. An article in *People's World* encouraged people to join People's Songs in order to help organize "the business of making music do a job that many and many a speech is unable to do." An article in the *Daily Worker* quoted a People's Songster's claim that "a song can often create a logic that a speech cannot do. It can make an embittered man creatively active again." Jackie Gibson Alper says, "I felt—and still feel—that song . . . can be a powerful way of reaching people who would close their ears to other approaches."[39]

From People's Songs' point of view, songs appealed strongly to emotions as well as to intellect and encouraged participation rather than passive listening. The act of singing together created a sense of unity and strength that might not otherwise exist. Dramatic examples of the latter function of song as a weapon include the use of songs to spread a strike, to drown out epithets of the opposition at a meeting, to build morale and attract publicity on a small picket line. For example, Mario Casetta points out that following an injunction to limit the picket line in the Hollywood technicolor strike, the union voted to have a People's Songster on the line with a union person. The singing of "You Can't Scare Me . . ." attracted a lot of publicity.[40]

More important than such limited tactical uses, however, was the ability of songs to move people, the expectation being that a permanent change in consciousness and action would result. Underlying the claims of how a song was superior to a speech was the assumption of many People's Songsters that songs would have the same effect on others as they had on them. Ronnie Gilbert states this explicitly: "I had a lot of faith in the effectiveness of songs because of my own experience of songs getting so deeply to me. . . . I expected them to have the same effect on others they had on me." Jackie Gibson Alper says she always enjoyed participating in musical, theatrical, and dance activities, and had the feeling that people who could not be reached in other ways would attend a cultural function "and be moved to thought and possibly even action enough to become involved in our struggles." David Sear says songs are encouraging; they offer a sense of togetherness. Fred Hellerman says, "Songs can heighten awareness, show people they're not alone in dealing with problems, [enable them to] establish contact and share concerns." Mario Casetta says People's Songs was a terrific morale-builder for the progressive movement. "It gives people courage to sing with people of like mind." Pete Seeger says that song functioned as a weapon by uniting people and clarifying issues. His comment on the effect of songs is that "great works of art have changed my whole life; they make you feel it's worth living."[41]

Many cultural workers who passed through People's Songs expressed boredom and irritation with Communist party politics. These same people—even the most anti-CP among them—were all committed to using song as a weapon. They were moved and excited by the songs through which they expressed their commitment to particular ideals and issues. For example, Ronnie Gilbert, who expressed above how deeply she was moved by songs, says she had problems with the CP from the start. She was turned off by meetings, by the Communists' sense of self-importance and knowing it all. "I am not a good organizational person," she says. "It's very hard for me to follow regulations or discipline. I tend to laugh a lot when I should probably be serious." Yet she is quick to add that her superficial contact with the party "doesn't mean I don't have a strong emotional attachment. . . . I am a believer . . . a faithkeeper, in certain basic tenets." Fred Hellerman expressed similar sentiments. He was not in the party for long, found it boring, and drifted in and out. "It was not something I really felt comfortable with. It struck me as a tremendous waste of a lot of energy and a lot of good will; people got lost in long doctrinaire speeches." Hellerman adds, "but this had little to do with certain standards one has and certain things that one feels make sense for the world."[42]

Others remember their contact with the CP similarly, as being characterized by boring meetings and long, doctrinaire speeches. Yet this did not lessen their commitment to the movement's ideals or their admiration of the party's work in many areas. Perhaps their instinctive distaste for party politics had the effect of strengthening their belief in the power of song compared to other forms of persuasion. Their experience was that singing could be profoundly political and a lot of fun, and thus have an important emotional effect on people. Youth, talent, temperament, and experience combined to convince People's Songsters that "singing these songs made you stronger . . . you could win a victory through the kind of uplifted mood that was created by creating and singing these songs."[43]

While it seems clear in retrospect that songs were most useful within the movement, at the time song as a weapon was viewed as a way to reach out to people outside the Communist movement. If the Communists' language and style—exemplified by political speeches or articles in the *Daily Worker*—were inaccessible to people, songs could be a more effective means of communication.[44] The difference between a song and a long, boring speech was not merely the fact that the former had music. The belief in song as a weapon implied a particular view of human beings and the process by which they became politicized. It implied that cultural products were important in shaping people's world views (hence the antipathy for popular music's "June-moon-croon" focus); that people had to be affected emotionally as well as intellectually in order to change their political outlook; and that participation rather than passive consumption was critical to the process of changing consciousness and acting on that changed point of view. Irwin Silber expressed this years later, commenting on the folk song revival: "[If] people will begin to do things for themselves, will sing for themselves, and will make their own music, then, in time, we can hope that people will try to make a better world for themselves as well."[45]

Though the connection between making one's own music and trying to create a better world may seem tenuous, it was not so far from People's Songsters' own experience of the power of song. What they failed to take into account in their belief in song as a weapon was the specific context in which they had developed their own musical and political outlook. They had either grown up within the movement culture or come to the Communist movement via cultural means during a particularly open, creative, exciting period. The coincidence of the Popular Front—including the relative tolerance of the CPUSA and the discovery of American folk music—with their youth, talent, and connection to the movement culture had shaped their political and musical viewpoint. But these conditions could not be duplicated in the postwar period. As the cold war developed, People's Songs lost its labor connections and began to be Red-baited by the press. In response, People's Songsters increased their determination and efforts, convinced that the need for their songs was greater than ever in such a context.

5

"Songs of Labor and the American People"

The first issue of the *People's Songs Bulletin* began: "The people are on the march and must have songs to sing. Now, in 1946, the truth must reassert itself in many singing voices."[1] The claim that the people were on the march was, of course, wishful thinking. The notion that the movement possessed "the truth" to which people had been denied access had been for years an important stimulus to American Communism. The idea that Communists knew "the truth" and had history on their side attracted and held many people to the movement. For others, this idea was a reason to suspect the Communists' motives. How could they be so certain and dogmatic? Had they told "the truth" about the Moscow trials?

In contrast to the sectarian political outlook of the Communist movement, which People's Songs shared, the latter's musical outlook was quite broad. In theory, the category of "people's songs" was all-inclusive. Any music that "the people" sang, listened to, or created was "people's music." Lee Hays expressed this in the *Bulletin:*

> It's still true that the only kind of music that I know how to sing is folk music. It's true, moreover, that the music I most enjoy singing, and sing best, is the music that I learned from Negro singers. But I know that my songs, plus those of Josh White, Woody Guthrie, John Jacob Niles, Carl Sandburg, The Almanacs, the Lomaxes, etc., don't constitute the only American music, nor all the real "people's" music . . .
>
> I believe in a people's music that will come from us all: from the jitterbugs, from the beer drinkers who put six million nickels a day in the juke boxes, from the dozens who write songs and send them in to

People's Songs Inc., from the guys and gals on picket lines, from the many singers on People's Songs Hootenannies, from all those of good faith who believe in the people.[2]

While some People's Songsters scorned popular music as mindless and corrupt, others liked it a lot. Ronnie Gilbert says she loved pop music as a kid. "My aesthetic sense was formed from other things besides folk music and the left movement. . . . I've been singing songs in public since I was four years old. . . . I sang on a children's radio program for three or four years, I sang in glee clubs at school. . . . My musical taste was not orthodox in terms of folk music or the left."[3]

"I did not think much about popular culture as a separate entity," says Mario Casetta. "I did then, and still do, like a number of things within pop culture. . . . I've always found pop songs that I liked—for whatever reason." Casetta says the purpose of People's Songs was not to replace pop music with folk music, since "pop music is what people like." The idea was to tap into the source of a singing America. "It was fun to get together to sing. We sang everything."[4]

Many People's Songsters probably shared Fred Hellerman's broad conception of people's culture. Hellerman liked pop culture so much that he played hooky from school in order to see Benny Goodman. Still, Hellerman found that folk music was "another world." Through the Almanacs, Woody Guthrie, and Leadbelly, Hellerman discovered a body of music that dealt with subjects other than love, music that was "liberating" and "exciting" because of the wide range of ideas, hopes, and frustrations it addressed.[5]

People's Songs was committed to more than the dissemination of traditional folk music, however. This was made clear in a response to letters from readers of the *Bulletin* who wanted to see more traditional folk songs printed. The editors pointed out that most famous folk songs and ballads were already available in commercial publications. "People's Songs is interested in folk songs, worksongs, and the best in the song tradition, but not to the exclusion of new songs. It works not as a folklore society, but as an organization serving the cultural needs of the people—in songs. There is a body of People's Songs which the commercial publications neglect, for obvious reasons. For the same obvious reasons, we are interested in them. So the best we can do for some of the folksong requests that come in is to refer you to the right publications."[6]

Even more important than spreading traditional folk songs, which represented the democratic heritage as People's Songs defined it, was creating a new body of folk-style political songs. Alan Lomax described the process: "At first I did not understand how these songs related to the traditional folk songs. . . . Slowly I began to realize that here was an emerging tradition that represented a new kind of human being, a new folk community composed of progressives and anti-fascists and union members. These folk, heritors of the democratic tradition of folklore, were creating for themselves a folk-culture of high moral and political content. These home-made songs of protest and affirmation shared the permanence of the people's tradition, but were most positive and more sharply critical than the familiar ballads."[7]

A wide variety of "people's songs" were printed in the *Bulletin*, from traditional folk songs, lullabies, and children's songs, to an occasional love song or show tune. Yet People's Songs clearly had a preference for certain types of songs. Folk-style songs with a political message dominated the writing, records, and performances of People's Songsters. The hope was that these new songs would become known and loved in their own right. The concern was neither with fitting the scholarly definition of a folk song nor with writing original songs as the Composers' Collective had set out to do. The style was set by Lee Hays and Woody Guthrie, writing new words to old tunes. Because of their accessibility and point of view, these songs would become "folk songs"—that is, "part of people's lives and a reflection of their thinking."[8]

People's Songs encouraged amateur songwriters along with professionals. The *Bulletin* implied that the primary qualification for becoming a people's artist was commitment. An article describing the formation of a People's Songs branch in Cleveland concluded with this message from organizer and song leader Bernie Asbel: "If anyone still believes that it takes genius or special training to write and sing people's songs—let them check up on Cleveland and find out they're wrong!"[9]

Critics decried Communist cultural activity on the grounds that political considerations negated aesthetic ones. For example, Arthur Schlesinger, Jr., claimed that "the wildly enthusiastic Communist claque for certain types of phony folk art has lowered the standards of many Americans not themselves party members or sympathizers."[10] Such concerns about the "general corruption of taste" promoted by the Communists were not always well founded, as the work of People's Songs demonstrates. The emphasis on commitment did not mean that People's Songs lacked critical standards.

It is true that People's Songsters—like most American Communists—did not view the working out of a new aesthetic as a primary task. As one member expressed it, there was a "natural aesthetic" that the group could not neglect if it hoped to influence the course of events. It was generally recognized that attention to aesthetics was necessary for political results. But questions of aesthetics were rarely discussed. Theoretical discussions of aesthetic standards were almost entirely absent from the *Bulletin* as well. The most sustained discussion of an aesthetic question consisted of two letters and one article arguing about the virtues and problems of singing English translations of songs. The editor concluded, with characteristic balance, that English translations were useful because they made songs accessible to the audience, but they should be "good" translations.[11]

The committee that screened songs to be printed in the *Bulletin* did not have guidelines by which to judge songs. Music editor Waldemar Hille and the other members relied on their own subjective standards to determine what they thought were good songs. Out of a pool of twenty or twenty-five songs each month, (and fifty or sixty during the Wallace campaign), the song-screening committee chose by consensus six or eight songs to be printed in each issue of the *Bulletin*. Anyone who submitted a song to the *Bulletin* received a form letter explaining what was being done with it. The song might be returned with a reminder that People's Songs was "interested mainly in topical songs." It might be kept for future use, or it might be published in the *Bulletin*, in which case permission to print it was requested. The last line of the form simply stated, "We are unable to use your song." In any case, there was no discussion with the writer about the quality of the song.[12]

Writers and performers also relied mainly on their own subjective standards in judging songs. One performer acknowledges that the question of aesthetics was a puzzle to him at the time. "I was either comfortable singing a song or I wasn't, it was right or wrong, but I had no words to describe why."[13] The few isolated attempts at consciously defining a good song were mainly variations on the theme of "a song is not a slogan." For example, an early issue of the *Bulletin* explained: "A song, to be a good song, to create desire on the listener's part to do just a little more about the struggles of his community, must have guts, meaning, and at the same time be handled in a skillful, articulate manner. Clichés put to a boogie beat still sound like clichés."[14]

The question of what made a good song had confronted the Almanac Singers in the early 1940s. The interaction of their varied styles of songwriting—if a less collective and spontaneous process than the myth would have it—led to the creation of some lasting songs. Joe Klein explains that Woody Guthrie, for example, did have a theory about how to write songs: "He took a classic high-culture position arguing against agitprop exhortation. You didn't have to slam people over the head; it was more artful and effective to *show* than to *tell*. He argued that writing a ballad was the ultimate test of a songwriter. Taking the story of an individual and turning it into a metaphor, like 'Tom Joad,' was far more difficult than just telling people to go out and join the union." Guthrie rarely stated such ideas explicitly, however. "Usually," says Klein, "he didn't have the patience or, perhaps, the conversational tools (or, perhaps, the guts) to explain his ideas about songwriting to the others."[15]

Even with the benefits of hindsight and years of experience, former People's Songsters still have difficulty putting into words their ideas about what makes a good song. Waldemar Hille says it's important to be flexible about what makes a good song. (Hille, who criticized Harry Belafonte when he came to the People's Songs office, says, "I guess I was a little sectarian.") Earl Robinson emphasizes the difference between a song and a slogan: "A song says it finer, more cleverly, deeply, profoundly, because it talks in terms of people's emotions and in the words that they use; more sharply, not clichéd." Mario Casetta echoes these sentiments, explaining that a good song is not an editorial, that it is not enough to set good intentions to music. A good song, he says, has to have "that indefinable something that catches people."[16]

To a great extent People's Songsters' judgments were utilitarian and pragmatic. This did not mean that any song that expressed the correct sentiment or point of view on paper was good. (The discarded songs in the People's Songs Library attest to this.) A good song was one that "worked." As Waldemar Hille states it, "We felt that when you really got a good song, people would respond. Every once in a while there would be . . . a 'bellringer,' and at other times there would be a question mark."[17] Audience response was the crucial aspect for judging the value of a song. Indeed, some members of the folk movement define a successful song as one that lasts because it catches on with audiences. Mario Casetta says that successful songs have "some element, a catch-phrase, an idea, a melodic line, something that sets them above and makes them last . . . people want to hear and sing them."[18] Weavers' manager Harold Leventhal developed his sense of what makes a good song while working for Tin Pan Alley in the late 1930s. Leventhal would watch Irving Berlin, who sat in the back of the audience at a Broadway show. Berlin knew he had a hit song if people came out humming. "People have to like it, hum and sing it," says Leventhal.[19]

In contrast, Irwin Silber claims that the popularity of a song was not of great concern at the time. What defines "people's songs" is not simply popularity, says Silber, but rather "the fact that they objectively represent what's in the best political interests of masses of people."[20] "People's songs" are not limited to what public opinion says are good songs, though of course the songs have to be aesthetically satisfying, says Silber. People's Songsters did think the ideas they expressed in song corresponded to the objective interests of the people. Still they looked to their audience for confirmation of those ideas and approval of the means of expressing them. Given the lack of discussion and consensus about a formal aesthetic, audience reaction was highly valued and its judgments were taken seriously. As one performer stated it, "The individual artist flew by the seat of his/her own pants and, as in pop culture, the reaction of the audience was the guide."[21]

Some songs which looked good on paper were discarded because they didn't work for an audience. Others for which the *Bulletin* song-screening committee lacked enthusiasm received more attention when they elicited a positive response from a live audience. A prominent example of this is "Passing Through," a song that the committee was not excited about initially. Set to a mountain tune, the song tells of "passing through" great historical moments, from Adam in the garden of Eden to Jesus on the cross to George Washington at Valley Forge, ending with

> I was at Franklin Roosevelt's side
> just a while before he died.
> He said "One world must come out of World War II.
> Yankee, Russian, white or tan,
> Lord a man is just a man,
> We're all brothers and we're only passing through."

When the Folksay group sang this song with a good response, its score went up higher, says Waldemar Hille.[22] The song was then printed in *Songs for Wallace*, becoming one of the more popular songs of the campaign. People's Songsters claimed to have different standards than the popular music industry for judging songs, yet their concern with audience response paralleled that of the industry, despite the difference in motives.

If audience response was critical to the success of people's songs, then it is important to determine who those audiences were and were not, and what kind of meaning they attached to the songs. The combination of the content and style of the songs, the talent of those who performed them, and the political context meant that people's songs were bound to find popularity within the Communist movement culture. As Art Shields expressed it, "When you are engaged in a . . . movement of struggle, then things related to that stimulate and please you."[23] But the songs were doomed to failure among the audience for whom they were primarily intended—labor unions.

To this day Pete Seeger maintains that People's Songs set out to create a "singing labor movement."[24] From the Communist point of view the organized labor movement would play the key role in carrying out a socialist revolution. People's Songs saw part of its role as helping to build unions, bringing working people that much closer to fulfilling their historic function. Earl Robinson, among others, says he totally supported labor and expected the labor movement to become revolutionary.[25]

The working class and the labor movement merged in People's Songsters' view of the world. Their high expectations of "labor" were focused on the CIO. Mario Casetta says, "I thought the labor movement—especially with the CIO in the lead—was the hope of the nation. I identified myself through singing and song-writing with the labor movement." As a child in the 1930s Ernie Lieberman thought "the CIO was 'our' union and its leaders were our heroes." Jerry Silverman, whose perception of labor was shaped by Woody Guthrie and union songs, says he had no doubt who the enemy was.[26]

People's Songsters had high expectations for their relationship with the labor movement, with which they were initially on good terms. One of the founding members of People's Songs was Palmer Webber, the educational director of the CIO. People's Songsters were proud of union songs and singing on picket lines. Work with the United Automobile Workers, production of a CIO songbook, an Amalgamated Clothing Workers' songbook, and a National Maritime Union filmstrip all heightened People's Songs expectations. In the early days, People's Songs even worked with a few AFL locals.

In its first year the *Bulletin* printed a number of articles from the CIO's political action committee which echoed People's Songs' faith in song as a weapon. For example, Alan Reitman, public relations director of CIO-PAC, explained that songs were useful in getting people out to vote: "Singing stirs emotion, and emotion makes people act, such action as carefully inspecting the issues and records of candidates, registering to vote, and voting on Election Day. It is here where People's Songs, which has been organized to bring the songs of the people to union choral groups and other people's organizations, can make a great contribution to our common cause."[27]

CIO-PAC's manual of techniques included a section on Music for Political Action, part of which was reprinted in the *Bulletin:*

Any rhythmic music will draw a crowd to a sound truck, but only a catchy song with a message written briskly and cleverly will send them home humming and singing it and spreading, in the most contagious and palatable form, the message you want them to carry.

Parodies of favorite old songs are the easiest to write and the most effective political songs. By taking a familiar folk song and writing new "socially significant" words for it—a satire on a political opponent or a treatment based on a legislative issue—you can create a potent weapon.[28]

People's Songsters were well aware of the role songs had played in the labor movement throughout United States history. Nineteenth-century workers expressed their grievances and their struggle for better conditions in such songs as "Eight Hours":

We mean to make things over,
We are tired of toil for naught
With but bare enough to live upon
And ne'r an hour for thought
We want to feel the sunshine
And we want to smell the flowers
We are sure that God has willed it
And we mean to have eight hours.
We're summoning our forces from the shipyard, shop, and mill.

Eight hours for work
Eight hours for rest
Eight hours for what we will[29]

Various occupational groups, most notably the miners, had traditionally sung about their working conditions and attempts to improve them. The IWW sang parodies of hymns and popular songs, expressing their displeasure with the capitalist system and urging workers to join together to change it. IWW member Ralph Chaplin wrote one of the best-known, lasting, and popular union songs to the tune of "John Brown's Body":

Solidarity Forever

When the union's inspiration through the workers blood shall run
There can be no power greater anywhere beneath the sun
Yet what force on earth is weaker than the feeble strength of one
For the union makes us strong.

Solidarity forever!
Solidarity forever!
Solidarity forever!
For the union makes us strong.[30]

The songs of Joe Hill had also encouraged workers to fight for better conditions. For example, in his hands the hymn "Sweet By-and-By" became "The Preacher and the Slave":

Long-haired preachers come out every night
Try to tell you what's wrong and what's right
But when asked about something to eat
They will answer with voices so sweet:

You will eat by and by
In that glorious land above the sky
Work and pray, live on hay
You'll get pie in the sky when you die.[31]

In the 1930s songs had been composed and sung by workers engaged in fierce battles for union recognition. During a miners' strike in "Bloody Harlan" (Harlan County, Kentucky) in 1932, Florence Reece wrote one of the most memorable songs of the period, "Which Side Are You On?"

Come all of you good workers
Good news to you I'll tell
of how the good old union
has come in here to dwell[32]

The chorus asks repeatedly, "Which side are you on?"

The heroic and tragic aspects of some of the 1930s battles were captured in such songs as Jim Garland's "The Death of Harry Simms," which tells the story of a young union organizer killed by the mine owners' hired gunmen. The last verse reports that

Harry Simms was killed on Brush Creek
In nineteen thirty-two
He organized the miners
Into the N.M.U.
He gave his life in struggle,
That was all that he could do
He died for the Union,
Also for me and you.[33]

Songs from the Almanac Singers' successful *Talking Union* album indicated that the tradition of expressing labor struggles in song did not end with the 1930s. The use of folk music forms—traditional, blues, hymns—is exemplified respectively by "Union Maid," "Talking Union," and "Get Thee behind Me, Satan," the lyrics of which were written by the Almanacs.[34]

Songs from all these sources were printed in the *Bulletin* and sung at hootenannies and, whenever possible, at union meetings and rallies and on picket lines. The songs started to become more widely known, but despite their growing popularity most of these songs were not embraced by the labor movement. Those that were adopted most likely lacked the meaning they had for People's Songsters and the Communist movement. Labor songs had increased resonance for Communist-oriented People's Songsters and their sympathetic left-wing audiences in the postwar period. The defeat of fascism and strengthening of democracy was connected in their minds to the inevitable victory of socialism. The songs functioned as reminders of past battles and exhortations on the need for ongoing struggle and vigilance. To union members, however, the songs probably had a very different meaning. Unions could sing "Which Side Are You On?" as an expression of solidarity without knowing about the intense battles in "Bloody Harlan" that inspired the song and contributed to its power. For union members, labor unity did not necessarily mean socialism.

Unions had experienced tremendous growth during the war. At the same time, the CPUSA reached its peak of respectability and influence in the labor movement. Cooperation in the war effort brought labor-Left unity, at least on the surface. The November 1943 CIO convention called World War II a "people's war of national liberation," in agreement with the Communist viewpoint. Most American workers supported the war and willingly carried out CIO head Phillip Murray's demand to "Heed the Call of your Commander-in-Chief and Work, Work, Work, Produce, Produce, Produce." The majority of workers stuck with the no-strike pledge and other measures that assured uninterrupted war production—measures that were supported wholeheartedly by the Communists.[35]

Below the surface, however, problems were brewing, suggesting that labor-Left unity would be short-lived. As the Communists supported the no-strike pledge and incentive pay, the collective bargaining process deteriorated, major corporations made high profits, and workers carried out wildcat strikes. Where Communists did stay in power in major unions, it was often because they muted or ignored Browder's line emphasizing wartime production at any cost.

The CIO accepted the government's wartime labor policy because of its own weaknesses, such as the lack of recognition or stable organizations in some basic industries. As unions grew during the war, they also became more dependent on government for their security. Labor's growing political influence, illustrated in the 1944 elections, came hand in hand with stronger ties to the Democratic party—ties that sealed the split between labor and the Left during the 1948 presidential campaign.

Increasing employment and unionization in the mass production industries brought other changes in the character of major unions. The new union members were not people who had experienced the great organizational struggles of the 1930s; they were, rather, workers who took out union cards as a condition of employment. Not only were the rank and file less union-minded, then, but the growth in union membership was accompanied by a proportionally greater expansion of CIO union bureaucracies. More than five million workers went on strike in 1946, yet these strikes were controlled by the CIO bureaucracy, as the national union leadership centralized its power. The postwar strikes indicated a return to pure-and-simple unionism. Management control of production was accepted in return for wages, pensions, and fringe benefits. Since the Communists had led in or acquiesced to most of these changes, they were not in much of a position to fight back as wartime nationalism became postwar anticommunism.

The CIO had adopted anti-Communist resolutions as early as 1939–40, with the cooperation of Communists in CIO leadership. More drastic action was taken in the postwar years as the issue of Communism became both a demagogic device used by labor leaders seeking power (such as Walter Reuther in the UAW) and an important measure of labor's relation to national attitudes. The anticommunism of the media, the government, employers, Catholic labor activists, and the CIO leadership led to a concern with "responsible unionism" in the late 1940s. The Left was purged from the CIO by a series of mergers, raids, and expulsions, and what emerged was a politically orthodox unionism characterized by a routinized, businesslike collective bargaining structure. "Responsible unionism" meant in effect dependence on government favor, the Democratic party, public opinion, and especially on a disciplined work force. In the long run this had negative effects on the internal structure of major unions, which became top-heavy, bureaucratized, and lacking in democratic representation. In the short run it meant the end of Communist influence in the labor movement.[36]

The 1946 CIO convention denounced Communism in a unanimous resolution. But the labor movement's sincerity was further tested in 1947 when the Taft-Hartley Act was passed, drastically restricting union organizing rights and activities. Taft-Hartley required union officials to sign loyalty oaths upon which NLRB bargaining rights were made contingent. The non-communist affidavits, according to Len de Caux, gave the Taft-Hartley Act "an anticommunist aura and betrayed its link with the Cold War foreign policy."[37] Labor took the hint, proving its anticommunism in terms of foreign policy questions. In October 1947 Soviet Communists presided over a conference of nine European parties which set up a Communist Information Bureau (Cominform) and issued a manifesto aimed at mobilizing opposition to the Marshall Plan. At the same time, the CIO convention in Boston welcomed Secretary of State George C. Marshall as its major guest speaker. Labor's repudiation of the Communists was clear, as the convention cheered Marshall's speech and unanimously adopted a resolution supporting Marshall's plan.[38]

Labor leaders further tested the rank and file's commitment to the cold war consensus during the 1948 presidential campaign. The CIO leadership supported Truman for president, disciplining members and locals for supporting or working with the Progressive party. When Harry Bridges of the International Longshoremen's and Warehousemen's Union refused to stop working for Wallace, he was fired as CIO regional director for northern California. The United Auto Workers executive board declared that the Progressive party was "a Communist Party maneuver designed to advance the foreign-policy interests of the

Soviet Union." The only major Left-led union to endorse Wallace was the Mine, Mill and Smelter Workers Union. While United Electrical leaders played an active role in the campaign as individuals, the union did not officially endorse Wallace; it left the question of whom to support up to its locals. Otherwise, only a few small unions, such as the Fur Workers and Marine Cooks and Stewards, gave Wallace their official endorsement. Michael J. Quill of the Transport Workers Union shifted from supporting to criticizing Wallace during the campaign. Some years before, the Transport Workers Union had bestowed an honorary life membership on Paul Robeson. Following the Wallace campaign, the union withdrew its invitation to Robeson to attend its annual convention. Robeson's absence, contrasting with his regular attendance for ten years, was another sign of the times.[39]

As the Communists' relationship with the labor movement deteriorated, People's Songs found its labor connections disappearing. Especially after 1947, People's Songs had little sustained contact with unions except the radical unions with Communist leadership: UE, Fur Workers, and Mine, Mill. The issue of anticommunism soon convulsed these Left-led unions as well. For example, UE, which had stayed with its proven—albeit Communist—leaders, was subjected to attacks by the electrical corporations, the federal government, and other unions. The union was expelled from the CIO in 1949. Not long after, UE broke with the Communists.[40]

People's Songs may have helped keep the Left in the unions as long as possible by contributing to strikes, picket lines, and organizing efforts, and by reminding labor of its own immediate history. Yet the labor movement never made use of People's Songs in a serious way. Performers found that singing to union audiences was a positive experience. "We sang for left-wing unions in idioms that a lot of workers didn't understand. They went from puzzled bemusement to joining in with a sense of pride—'Why, they're singing songs about us.' . . . But we weren't important to most sections of the labor movement, and totally unknown to most."[41] Singers rarely got beyond the left-wing unions, and even there the songs were not seen as important. Besides, unions viewed songs as entertainment, while People's Songsters had the illusion that they were providing political education. The assumption that the labor movement would embrace both their musical idiom and their political message turned out to be seriously mistaken.

Few People's Songsters had organic ties with the labor movement. Some came from working-class backgrounds, often of immigrant parents. But they were more assimilated and upwardly mobile than their parents. What connections they had with labor were based on the Communist movement. Their high expectations of labor support and militance came less from concrete experience than from an ideological, romanticized view of workers and unions. Frank Hamilton's outlook was not atypical: "I romanticized shipping out with the N.M.U. or singing for labor unions and identified with the radical efforts in labor unions. . . . My only real identification was my association with the Musician's Union which was disillusioning."[42] The style and content of people's songs continued to have more meaning to Frank Hamilton and the other People's Songsters than they did to the labor movement. Work with unions generated great hope and excitement among People's Songsters, but these opportunities dwindled as labor began to sever its connections with the Left.

The lack of labor support for People's Songs must be understood in the context of the unions' postwar search for stability and respectability. This search coincided with, and took the form of, the developing anti-Communist consensus. While Pete Seeger and People's Songs "reckoned without the cold war," the labor movement was under tremendous pressure to rid itself of the stigma of Communism.[43] There was no militant movement of labor comparable to the IWW or the early CIO in which workers were taking a stand. In the context of routinized collective bargaining sessions, songs could not perform the morale-building function they had played at rallies, meetings, demonstrations, and picket lines in the 1930s. But the point is not that unions were resistant to singing per se; they were concerned with declaring their independence from the Left. Instead of supporting the efforts of People's Songs, unions began to publish their own songbooks. One former People's Songster says this was because the unions "did not want to be held hostage to the fact that this singing tradition was associated with the left and the Communists."[44]

The importance of such political issues as the Marshall Plan and the Wallace campaign in determining labor-Communist relations reveals the problem with the conception of a "singing labor movement." People's Songsters were as intransigent as the rest of the Communist movement on political issues. They did not merely want labor unions to sing. They expected workers to sing songs with a particular content, as part of a broad progressive movement. Workers were not singing about the class war or the cold war in the way People's Songsters had assumed they would. "Song of My Hands" was popular on the left, but it was not sung in labor unions.

Song of My Hands

What is the value of my two hands
Appraise them as you've done before
They built your factories, tilled your lands
They made your riches, and they'll make more
What will you pay for my hands?

Calculate carefully,
Ponder it well,
And remember this when you do
That my two hands
Are mine to sell;
They made your machines
They can stop them, too,
That is the power of my hands.

My two hands are mighty hands
They're hard, they're strong, they're Free
In all the world there's no man
can buy them in slavery.[45]

It was a forecast of things to come that the October 1947 issue of the *Bulletin* no longer listed Palmer Webber as a member of the board of directors. There was little labor support for People's Songs' "Communist" or "Popular Front" views, which were becoming indistinguishable to a nation dominated by cold war hysteria.

In fact, the *Bulletin* was not filled with Communist dogma and rhetoric, nor did it posit a Communist solution to the problems it addressed. While it expressed sincere hopes for "stronger unity between all people . . . for peace, for a better life for all, and for the brotherhood of man," it did not present any more specific vision of an alternative social system.[46] After all, few People's Songsters had a vision of what the United States or the world would look like under socialism, or of what it would take to achieve this transition. They expected that the extension of democracy would somehow lead to socialism. In the meantime, they saw the task of People's Songs as helping out in short-term campaigns to build unions, fight racism, and push for jobs and price controls. People's Songs' activity, like much of the work of the Communist movement, was based on this concern with immediate issues.

If the *Bulletin* did not express a Communist point of view per se, it did express the "Popular Frontism" of its founders. In essence, "Popular Frontism" meant not being exclusive, involving "all the people" in the defense of democratic rights. A typical statement of People's Songs' purpose was that it sought to use "every musical means available to bring the democratic message to the American people."[47] An important part of "the democratic message" was in songs of the American past. Singing folk and folk-style songs about protest movements, workers, political events, and leaders was one way of returning the democratic heritage to the American people. These songs reaffirmed People's Songsters' belief in "The people, yes the people" and their potential to create their own destiny.

When asked to express his ultimate message, Pete Seeger once paraphrased two lines from "John Henry":

> And before you let that steam drill beat you down
> Die with that hammer in your hand.[48]

John Henry symbolized the power of the workers whose labor had built America as well as the contributions of black people to enriching American culture. His larger-than-life heroism represented the dignity and determination of the people. John Henry's battle to assert his humanity against great odds made him a powerful symbol both of the democratic past and of hope for the future.

Oppressed groups throughout American history created songs to express discontent with their conditions and the promise of a brighter future. Opponents of slavery sang the Negro spiritual "Didn't My Lord Deliver Daniel": "Didn't my Lord deliver Daniel, And why not every man." And they sang of following "The Drinking Gourd," the Big Dipper, north to freedom: "The old man is a-waiting for to carry you to freedom, If you follow the drinking gourd." Nineteenth-century immigrants protested employment discrimination in "No Irish Need Apply." Populists concerned with the plight of small farmers sang "The Farmer Is the Man." People's Songs proudly printed such songs, which had challenged the dominant culture in the past, expecting the protest sentiment expressed in these songs to strike a chord in people dissatisfied with current conditions.[49]

Groups of workers who protested and fought for control over their working conditions were also celebrated in song. The introduction to "The Buffalo Skinners," a cowboy song collected by John Lomax, indicates what such songs meant to People's Songsters:

> We always like to point out this song to folksingers of the "purist" kind who claim they would sing "the nice old ballads but not these modern propaganda songs." We suspect that they don't realize that half the best old songs were red hot propaganda in their day . . . take this "Buffalo Skinners," one of the finest of all cowboy songs: first, the singer admits to a state of unemployment (don't mention the word); then he insists upon free transportation (portal-to-portal pay, no less!); he complains of working conditions, and then when the boss reneges on pay, he kills him (the un-American Committee would have us all in the pokey for writing such a song like this now, we're positive).[50]

Accompanying this introduction and the song was an article about the history of workers expressing grievances in song. The article, "Before the Unions Came," explicitly presented American history as a history of class struggle (a rare instance in which this phrase appeared in the *Bulletin*). The article claimed that "J. Parnell Thomas to the contrary, the class struggle was not invented by the CIO—or by the Comintern. Folksong and folklore alike bear testimony to conflicts between masters and men long before the appearance of unions or 'reds.'"[51]

Another aspect of the democratic heritage was expressed in songs commemorating historical events and figures. For example, an early American ballad celebrating the Boston tea party was introduced as "one of the best of all songs of America's Revolutionary War."[52] People's Songsters' identification with the

American past and its folk songs was also explicitly communicated by their printing of the "Star-Spangled Banner." The song was reclaimed for the people in the following terms: "The fact that the tune of this, one of America's first revolutionary songs, was an old drinking song proves that it came from the people and shall forever belong to the people."[53]

As Communists had done during the Popular Front years, People's Songs turned to the revolutionary American past to express the idea that "Communism is twentieth-century Americanism." Political figures such as Thomas Jefferson and Abraham Lincoln became folk heroes, revered for their influential and inspirational commitment to liberty and justice for all the people. "Jefferson and Liberty" was sung in great earnest, with Jefferson's campaign being compared to Henry Wallace's as a quest to protect the rights of common people. The flavor of this early election song is illustrated in the first verse and the chorus:

> The gloomy night before us flies,
> The reign of terror now is o'er;
> Its gags, inquisitors and spies,
> Its herds of harpies are no more.
>
> Rejoice, Columbia's sons, rejoice
> To tyrants never bend the knee
> But join with heart and soul and voice
> For Jefferson and Liberty[54]

"Abe Lincoln," written by Alfred Hayes and Earl Robinson (with a chorus taken from an address by Abraham Lincoln), celebrated the commitment to liberty and democracy that defined Lincoln's popular image:

> Now old Abe Lincoln, a great big giant of a man was he (Yes Sir!)
> He was born in an old log cabin and he worked for a living (Splittin' rails!)
> Now Abe he knew right from wrong
> For he was honest as the day is long
> And these are the words he said:
>
> "This country with its institutions belongs to the people who inhabit it."
> This country with its Constitution belongs to us who live in it.
> "Whenever they shall grow weary of the existing Government,

They can exercise their constitutional right of amending it,
Or their revolutionary right to dismember or overthrow it."[55]

Songs were also composed about the most recent inspirational leader who had been on the side of the people—Franklin Delano Roosevelt. "Ballad of FDR" was introduced as follows:

> We remember Roosevelt because we remember the best years of our lives as a nation and a people.
>
> In the New Deal, we found ourselves culturally, as well as politically.
>
> We had the beginning of a great people's culture, in theater, art, literature, music—all the expressions of our talent and our hope for a better land . . .
>
> We remember Roosevelt, and revere his memory as an inspirited leader with faith in our own ability to make a living people's culture.[56]

People's Songsters' view of the democratic American past was complemented by their vision of a world future based on socialism, peace, and people's culture. Far from being contradictory, Communism would be a natural outgrowth of Americanism. The security and the free and full development of each individual, the ultimate aim of communism in theory, also seemed to be the promise of American democratic rhetoric and traditions. Postwar America's prosperity and power, harnessed in the interests of the people, could usher in the "century of the common man" on a global scale.

For People's Songsters, world freedom songs were a means of promoting unity, understanding, and cooperation. They had the potential to educate people about the political struggles and cultural expressions of other lands. Celebrating freedom fighters of the past and present, songs served as emotional reminders that the battle against fascism was not over. To people in the Communist movement the songs represented shared experiences, pride in those who had fought for their beliefs, and a reaffirmation of those beliefs. Yet People's Songs found little support in the postwar political context for its attempt to project national and Allied unity during World War II into an international future of peace and cooperation.

Many liberals in the postwar years were concerned about defeating fascism in the United States and abroad. They feared economic disaster, which they thought would encourage the development of an incipient native fascism. They were unhappy with the Truman administration's policy in Europe, which often encouraged the remnants of fascism. While the United States government did little to help displaced Jews find a home, it worked with people and groups once close to the Nazis in Germany, tolerated the Franco government in Spain, and supported the right wing in the Greek Civil War.

Given these concerns, one might expect that liberals who drew upon the ideas of the late 1930s to develop a vision of a "worldwide New Deal" would join in singing international freedom songs. People's Songs printed songs from the Spanish Civil War ("Viva La Quince Brigada," "Freiheit"), from the concentration camps ("Peat Bog Soldiers"), from World War II partisans ("French Partisan Song"), and from the Greek resistance ("Embross Elas," "Laokratia"). They also printed songs in support of strengthening the United Nations: "United Nations make a chain, Every link is freedom's name, Keep your hand on the plow, hold on!" Yet despite their antifascism, their international vision, and their initial faith in the United Nations to help solve the problems of the postwar period, liberals did not join the Left in singing these songs.[57]

As historian Alonzo Hamby points out, "In large part, the story of the liberal movement in the postwar years involved the discarding of a fundamental assumption—belief in the Popular Front and in the unity of the anti-fascist left."[58] Americans for Democratic Action (ADA) led American liberalism toward its new identity, in which the important dividing line became one's attitude toward the Russians abroad and toward American Communists at home. The Marshall Plan thereby became an important test for liberals, as it was for labor. It was supported by many liberals who hoped for European rehabilitation and unity (though some criticized it for avoiding the United Nations). According to the liberal argument, if the Russians rejected the Marshall Plan, that was their problem. By contrast, the Communist-oriented Left, along with many progressives who supported Wallace, viewed the Marshall Plan as a containment device which would further divide the world while propping up fascists.

Given the postwar political context and the historical twists and turns of American Communism, People's Songsters should not have been surprised that appeals for "world freedom" were met with suspicion. The history of American Communist internationalism was ambiguous. In certain periods it meant calling attention to important world problems and making sacrifices for the freedom of others. At the same time, however, internationalism meant that following the lead of the Soviet Union and identifying with foreign struggles took precedence over addressing the contradictions of American life. It was of course the latter form of internationalism, the identification with the Soviet Union, which the government and media emphasized in their accusations of "un-Americanism." The goals of the Communist Left were further discredited and distorted in the minds of the American people by liberal intellectuals' equation of communism with fascism.[59]

Yet People's Songs' international songs were not revolutionary or Communist for the most part. There were some revolutionary songs from other lands printed in the *Bulletin.* "Kevin Barry," for example, celebrated the martyrdom of a young Irish soldier who fought against the British in the 1916 revolution.

> Shoot me like an Irish soldier
> Do not hang me like a dog
> For I fought for Ireland's freedom
> On that dark September morn
> All around that little bakery
> Where we fought them hand to hand
> Shoot me like an Irish soldier
> For I fought to free Ireland.[60]

Barry's refusal to turn informer to free himself took on added significance to the Left as the House Committee on Un-American Activities began its campaign to convince people to "name names."[61]

Bertolt Brecht and Hanns Eisler's song of the "United Front" explicitly stated that "the liberation of the working class is the job of the workers alone."[62] Yet revolutionary songs were the exception, rather than the rule. It was not simply the content of the songs that made People's Songs unable to reach labor and the American people. The American Communist movement's loyalty and right to exist was being questioned, and People's Songs was accused of being a Communist front. Those progressives or liberals who might have sympathized with the sentiments expressed by People's Songs were not eager to acknowledge any similarities in outlook, past or present. In the context of intense anticommunism, the singing of antifascist and partisan songs of many lands was viewed as subversive and un-American activity.[63]

The topical songs that dominated the *Bulletin* also failed to reach a mass audience. Many of the issues addressed in songs, from prices and housing to peace and civil rights, concerned people outside the Communist movement. Yet labor and the American people did not embrace these songs as their own. The songs did not call for a socialist revolution in the United States; rather, they addressed issues on which it became more and more sensitive and risky to speak out as the cold war took hold.

Some topical songs expressed or promoted the idea of class struggle. Two songs from England focused on the differences in class interests between workers and capitalists. The chorus to "I Water the Workers Beer," ran:

I'm the man, the very fat man, that waters the workers beer
I'm the man, the very fat man, that waters the workers beer
And what do I care if it makes them ill,
If it makes them terribly queer?
I've a car and a yacht and an aer-o-plane,
and I waters the workers beer.[64]

"Pity the Downtrodden Landlord" began this way:

Please open your hearts and your purses
To a man who is misunderstood
He gets all the kicks and the curses
Tho' he wishes you nothing but good
He wistfully begs you to show him
You think he's a friend not a louse
So remember the debt that you owe him
The landlord who lends you his house.

So pity the downtrodden landlord
And his back that is burdened and bent
Respect his grey hairs,
Don't ask for repair,
And don't be behind with the rent![65]

One of the more popular people's songs, which matched the above in sarcastic attacks on the bosses, was "Put It on the Ground":

> For men who own the industries
> I'm sheddin' bitter tears;
> They never made a single dime
> In over thirty years
> In over thirty years, my boy,
> In over thirty years
> Not one thin dime, in all that time,
> In over thirty years . . . ohhh . . .
>
> Put it on the ground
> Spread it all around
> Dig it with a hoe
> It will make your flowers grow![66]

For the most part, however, topical songs confronted specific issues. One immediate concern addressed by People's Songs was inflation. An early issue of the *Bulletin* boasted a special supplement on saving the federal Office of Price Administration. Other issues included such songs as "High Price Blues" and the popular "A Dollar Ain't a Dollar":

> I was feeling kind of hungry,
> So I thought I'd buy some bread,
> And I went into the corner grocery store
> I took out the usual money,
> But the grocer shook his head,
> 'Cause a dollar ain't a dollar anymore.
>
> Oh, a dollar bill don't buy what it used to,
> don't buy what it used to,
> don't buy what it used to.
> Oh, a dollar bill don't buy what it used to,
> 'Cause a dollar ain't a dollar anymore.[67]

The problem of the postwar housing shortage was addressed in "I'm A-Looking for a Home" and "I Want a Home," among others. Some of the more popular people's songs attacked the conservative character of Congress, as in "Listen, Mr. Bilbo":

Listen, Mr. Bilbo, wherever you may be,
I'll give you a lesson in history;
Listen while I tell you that the foreigners you hate
Are the very same people made America great.[68]

Other political issues addressed by People's Songs made the group more vulnerable to anti-Communist attacks. One such issue was peace. People's Songs was not the only group concerned about how the atomic bomb would affect the world's future. Yet the group received little response to songs which called for "peace in the world or the world in pieces." As the cold war developed, speaking out for peace came to be viewed as being pro-Soviet.[69] There were American Communists whose commitment to peace stemmed primarily from their concern with the welfare of the Soviet Union, as it had during the period of the Nazi-Soviet pact. Yet many others, including People's Songsters, were more concerned with what the bomb meant for the human race, given the possible consequences of "the next war." A peace song written by Harry Schachter and Earl Robinson in 1940 was revived during the postwar period. "The Spring Song" became popular on the Left:

There could be a celebration in the spring
Why destroy creation in the spring
With the common bond of labor, do I have to hate my neighbor
If he's from another nation in the spring?[70]

While People's Songsters urgently sang "The Spring Song," "Talking Atomic Blues," and "Walk in Peace," those who might have shared their desire for world peace failed to join them.

Civil rights was another important issue distorted by the cold-war frame of reference. Communists had played a major role in civil rights battles in the 1930s, fighting for an antilynching bill, defending black rights in the CIO, and publicizing the Scottsboro case. Civil rights issues received further attention in the 1940s as black people connected the fight against the Nazis abroad with that against Jim Crow at home. Race riots broke out in response both to segregation in the armed forces and to black mobility during the war. Communists were often accused of exploiting legitimate grievances for their own ends, using the civil rights issue to recruit blacks. Certainly they were interested in winning people over to their cause, even as the party line on the "Negro question" kept changing. As Bert Cochran points out, however, charges of Communist manipulation are misleading. "The purpose was not personal aggrandizement or self-seeking: they . . . courageously championed the Black cause when to do so was as popular or rewarding as the championship of Christianity in the time of Nero. If they fought fanatically and often unscrupulously to win people to the Party line, it was because they thought that on that line humanity was destined to advance to its salvation."[71]

Mark Naison has written about how the CPUSA became a key center of political initiative and cultural leadership among Harlem intellectuals during the Popular Front. The black middle class was attracted by the party's interracial strategies, internationalism, and cultural policies. The latter, based on a view of black culture as politically progressive, led to pioneering efforts to secure institutional support for the black arts and to end discrimination in sports, education, and other areas.

The CPUSA presented black culture and cultural interchange between the races as defining features of the American experience, to be celebrated and dramatized. "The uniqueness of this perspective cannot be emphasized enough," says Naison. "Historically, opponents of civil rights had argued that racial equality meant cultural degeneracy, that Black culture embodied a barbarism that would undermine American civilization if Blacks were not prohibited from 'social intercourse' with Whites and excluded from positions of political power. Popular Front critics turned this argument on its head, arguing that the distinctive culture of Blacks contributed to much that was vital and original in American life and that their full emancipation would strengthen the entire nation."[72]

Alan Lomax developed this argument in relation to black folk music. Every area of American folk song, from the folk hymn to the blues, was affected by black folk music, according to Lomax. The merging of West African and British folk traditions accounted for the unique quality of American folk song and revealed a unity that undercut surface tensions. Because of its popularity among blacks and whites and because of its emphasis on the theme of freedom, black folk music had a profound influence on American culture. Extending this influence, said Lomax, would bring Americans closer to realizing the promise of their democratic traditions.[73]

A similar vision connecting the struggle for racial equality with a movement of cultural regeneration stimulated the career of Paul Robeson. Robeson was an influential figure for many People's Songsters. He spoke of singing back to the people the songs they themselves had created. He dramatized in song the richness of the American cultural heritage. As an internationally renowned actor and singer, he won worldwide recognition for Negro folk songs which, he said, expressed the spirit of oppressed people everywhere. Robeson's career was virtually destroyed by the government's attempts to silence him in the postwar period. Yet he continued to live his belief that "my song is my weapon," expressing his determination in performances, sponsorship of organizations (including People's Songs), and work for the Wallace campaign.[74]

People's Songs' concern with black folk music and civil rights struggles was expressed in a number of ways. A significant portion of People's Songs' work was devoted to black music, black artists, and the theme of freedom. Civil rights was a major focus of songs, articles, performances, and work in the Wallace campaign. Field hollers, work songs, hymns, and spirituals were presented as black contributions to American culture. Songs expressed themes ranging from African roots to the battle against slavery to current struggles against Jim Crow.[75] Big Bill Broonzy sang his "Black, Brown, and White Blues": "Now if you's white, you's right, but if you's brown, stick around, and if you's black, oh brother, Git back, git back, git back." Josh White sang one of the more popular topical songs, "The Free and Equal Blues":

> I was down in the St. James Infirmary
> And I saw some plasma there
> And I up and ask the doctor
> Was the donor dark or fair?
> Well the Doc he laughed a great big laugh
> He laughed right in my face
> He said a molecule is just a molecule son
> And the damn thing has no race

And that was news, yes that was news
That was very, very, very special news
And ever since that day
I got those Free and Equal Blues.[76]

People's Songsters' determination to print and sing these songs was a significant political statement. Such singing evoked cries of outrage and attempts at suppression in a context in which segregationists and others connected white supremacy and anticommunism. In spite of attacks by government, media, and others, People's Songs maintained its commitment to racial equality, thereby providing a determined link between civil rights battles of the 1930s and the movement that began in the 1950s. The September 1948 issue of the *Bulletin* printed "We Will Overcome" (the song that later became "We Shall Overcome") with a comment by Zilphia Horton: "Its strong emotional appeal and simple dignity never fails to hit people. It sort of stops them cold silent."[77]

While civil rights was controversial, civil liberties was the issue which most clearly revealed postwar American Communists' determination and isolation. There were people who sympathized with the other topical issues addressed by People's Songs, but defending the civil liberties of Communists was a priority of very few people who were not themselves Communists. Songs that criticized the witch-hunters, such as "Is There a Red under Your Bed?" and "The Unfriendly Nineteen" (about the House Committee on Un-American Activities questioning of Hollywood screenwriters) made clear People's Songs' opposition to anticommunism. Such songs as "Red Boogie," which told the story of a worker kicked out of a maritime union for his "Red" sympathies, were popular on the Left but did not reach a broader audience. As abuses of civil liberties increased and people became more intimidated about speaking out on certain issues, People's Songsters refused to be silenced.[78] They fought back in songs that reflected their sectarian outlook and their isolation on the one hand, their courage and determination on the other.

The songs created, promoted, and distributed by People's Songs were in some sense "songs of labor and the American people" in terms of their musical origins and their concerns.

Some songs were promoted and distributed for their historical value, while others were written to serve an immediate purpose and were valued for their timeliness. Though many of these songs did not last and never reached a mass audience, their worth is still defended by People's Songsters. David Sear claims that "the songs were awfully good then for what they were needed for." Pete Seeger still insists that "even a song that lasts one day isn't a waste of time. If it's a good song and does a job, it's worth making up." Seeger says the *Bulletin* illustrates "bravery and honesty" along with "amateurishness." Irwin Silber points out that the *Bulletin* is a less-than-adequate reflection of what was a living movement. While it contains some "doggerel," this does not detract from the point that the songs did work in various ways, addressing issues and expressing a point of view while encouraging others to do the same. Jerry Silverman says the songs in the *Bulletin* are worth their weight in gold. Those that aren't at a high level musically are still "priceless social documents." In other words, it is the context in which and the purposes for which the songs were written—despite their limited audience and uneven quality—that makes them valuable.[79]

Despite their concern about important issues and despite the broad content of the songs, People's Songs was unable to reach labor and the American people. This was due in part to People's Songs' political sectarianism and naiveté, ties to the Communist movement, and expectations. The songs and articles in the *Bulletin* reflect People's Songsters' expectation of a broad progressive movement. They were unable and unwilling to admit that their assumptions were wrong. There was no postwar Popular Front; the people were not poised to receive People's Songs' version of "the democratic message"; and songs could not in and of themselves *create* the kind of movement for which People's Songs had hoped.

At the same time, People's Songsters' inability to reach their intended audience had more to do with broad historical and political changes over which they had no control. The cold war and anticommunism, changes in the labor movement, and the Communist movement's return to orthodoxy all played a significant part in limiting People's Songs' audience. The New Deal and Popular Front sentiments expressed enthusiastically in songs of the American past illustrated how out of sync People's Songs was as the cold war developed. It was not clear to People's Songsters at the time that the new definition of "Americanism," spreading from the centers of government to labor and the American people, would doom their efforts to disseminate and popularize their songs and their message.

Instead of seeing their songs returning the democratic heritage to the American people, educating them on the issues, and encouraging them to create their own culture, People's Songsters found that their major impact in the short run was on the Communist movement culture itself. The songs became first and foremost songs of the Communist movement, helping to strengthen the movement culture as the movement itself declined. People's Songs simultaneously increased the movement's determination and reflected its growing isolation. These processes were manifest in the group's two major musical forums—the hootenanny and the Wallace campaign.

6

"We Were Close to Changing the World": The People's Songs Hootenanny

In 1946 *Fortune* magazine quoted Woody Guthrie's definition of hootenannies as "song fests named after Hootin' Annie, a legendary queen whose lusty powers stirred the lumber workers." The hootenanny received national attention, but *Fortune* readers were not likely to have understood how Guthrie's tongue-in-cheek remark suggested the significance of the hootenanny, an institution that grew out of a long tradition of "song fests" which had helped to unify social movements throughout American history.[1] In the summer of 1941 Woody Guthrie and Pete Seeger attended a singing party in Seattle which the locals called a "hootenanny." The Almanac Singers borrowed the word and in the fall of 1941 held Sunday afternoon "hootenannies" that enabled them to pay the rent on their Manhattan townhouse. These gatherings grew along with the Almanacs' popularity. In 1946 People's Songs began to use "hootenanny" as the title for its musical programs. As hootenannies moved to larger settings, such as Carnegie Hall in New York, People's Songs began to rely on these events to raise money for other activities.

People's Songs disseminated folk and topical songs, encouraging people to participate in writing and singing such songs. In terms of the group's hope to create a significant alternative to the passive consumption of Tin Pan Alley's "June-moon-croon" products, the hootenanny was People's Songs' greatest success at the time. Beyond providing financial support, the hootenanny enabled People's Songs to circumvent the "music monopoly of

Broadway and Hollywood" and reach the public with "people's music."[2]

A People's Songs' manual called *How to Plan a Hootenanny* indicates the intentions and the main characteristics of a hoot. The manual emphasized, first of all, making the hootenanny accessible. It advised keeping ticket prices low in order to attract the greatest number of people. Use of a variety of song material was the ideal: "'Something Old, Something New, Something Borrowed, Something Blue.' This requisite for a bride is a good guide to planning a Hootenanny program. It should have old folk songs, new topical material, something borrowed from the culture of another country, and some form of blues or boogie."[3] A hoot was also supposed to include a variety of cultural forms. Folk and interpretive dancing, story telling, and skits were recommended as exciting additions to a hoot, yet singing clearly predominated.

Hootenannies were characterized by variety in other ways as well. While a hoot might feature some well-known performers, new young artists were also given opportunities to perform. Songs aimed at stimulating mass singing were the trademark of a hoot, but the manual advised that individual performers be given a chance to show off their specialties.

People's Songs' hoots ideally served to entertain and educate people, reaching them on an emotional and intellectual level. A program was often focused on a particular theme with a clear educational purpose. "Every hootenanny should have a theme," stated the manual. "Hootenannies serve a useful social function by dealing with current issues."[4] Different People's Songs' branches used "Union," "Un-American," "Free and Equal," and numerous other themes. Yet not every hoot, nor all material at a given hoot, was concerned with political issues.

The live, spontaneous music at a hootenanny contrasted with the trend toward professional recorded music. People came together to enjoy a collective experience, as opposed to individually "consuming" the music in the privacy of their own homes. The passivity encouraged—and often demanded—by popular music (in which, Adorno argued, "the composition listens for the listener") was broken down at the hootenanny.[5] The essential feature of a hoot, as far as form was concerned, was that everyone participated in making music. People were expected to lend their voices to the sound and spirit being created. The emphasis on audience participation in the form of mass singing made as important a political statement as the content of the songs. The clear message was that meaningful culture and politics were created by "the people."

Through the hootenanny, People's Songsters challenged the conception of culture as passive entertainment separate from the rest of life. They viewed culture as an integral part of life that could help people understand the world and develop their creative capacities. Pete Seeger later expressed the idea this way: "Somehow, somewhere along the line, Americans must learn, as our grandparents knew, that it is fun to create for yourself. . . . Ultimately, rank-and-file participation in music goes hand in hand with creativity on other planes—arts, sciences, and yes, even politics."[6]

Not all that took place at a hootenanny was spontaneous. Over time, as higher musical standards were employed in the planning process, hoots became more professional. The abilities of particular performers and the quality of particular songs (the latter judged by their content and their usefulness in group singing) were recognized in the planning of a hoot. There were discrepancies, then, between an ideal and an actual hootenanny as far as variety of form and level of spontaneity, but these did not detract from the institution's real and symbolic significance for People's Songs.

Those who participated still remember the musical and political excitement of the postwar hootenannies. Ben Dobbs characterizes them as "entertaining and exciting. I'd go to one now if it were advertised, no matter who was putting it on." Earl Robinson describes the hootenanny this way: "It wasn't that nobody was starred—everybody was starred. There were amateurs and pros, new songs and old ones, dance, poetry, and a lot of group singing. It was magic, an event." Mario Casetta describes the development of the Los Angeles hoots, at which he played master of ceremonies. The first hoot was held in a small place in Hollywood. The audience joined in on almost every song, and the hoot was a smash success. From then on, hoots were held almost once a month. A format developed with everyone sitting on stage and taking turns getting up and singing, with the audience joining in. Casetta says: "People used to go crazy for these things. It was just fantastic. . . . I lived, ate, slept, breathed People's Songs and we would have these incredible hoots." David Sear characterizes the hootenannies at Irving Place in New York City as "the most exciting musical experiences of my life in many ways." They were "a tremendous emotional experience. They were mind-boggling. I've never experienced anything like them." Jerry Silverman explains the social, political, and musical importance of hootenannies in the lives of young "people's artists." In New York City the first fall hootenanny became a summer-camp reunion. It was an exciting chance to perform and hear others perform. "There was a spirit that was generated in the hootenannies . . . that was absolutely uplifting," says Silverman. "It was at those moments, probably, that I thought we were close to changing the world."[7]

On a smaller scale and in an urban setting a hootenanny served functions similar to those of a nineteenth-century rural camp meeting. The parallels between the hootenanny and the Methodist-Baptist camp meeting are highly illuminating. The point is not to focus on the religious fervor which emanated from such gatherings—though that similarity should not be overlooked and is, ultimately, important—but rather to indicate the role of such institutions in strengthening the bonds of a movement. In the setting of a camp meeting or a hootenanny, the culture of a social movement was developed and revealed. Songs were a crucial part of the form and substance of these gatherings.

Even in its origins in the early nineteenth century, the camp meeting was more than a religious gathering; it was a major social event of frontier life. An itinerant preacher indicated one social function of camp meetings—i.e., as courting grounds—by changing the words of a chorus from "I want to get to heaven, my long-sought rest" to "I want to get to heaven with my long short dress."[8] The hootenanny served a similar function as a meeting place for those committed to a common ideal. Though serious in purpose, hoots were designed to be fun social events.

With a few exceptions, the main features of a camp meeting parallel those of a hootenanny. While it is difficult to measure the success rate of "conversion," the ultimate goal, the process that took place was strikingly similar. The form and content served to bind people together and mark their separation from the dominant culture. First of all, a camp meeting and a hootenanny offered a sense of community among people of a particular sect. Second, both involved expressions of faith in a certain type of "salvation," an inevitable new social order. Third, all such gatherings featured audience participation, particularly in singing songs that expressed their beliefs.

Dickson Bruce has described the camp meeting as a significant feature of "plain-folk" religion: "Everything that went on in a camp-meeting was of the plain-folk's devising and grew out of a response to their needs." The camp meeting was the setting for people with shared values and ideas to form a religious community. The sense of community was further enhanced by the conversion process itself, in which formerly important social distinctions were no longer recognized. Blacks and whites, men and women, aged and young intermingled and exchanged roles, violating the normal customs, for "only when the old world and the old ways of relating to others were no longer valid could a new world . . . assume its rightful place."[9]

Camp-meeting practices were intended to assure the participants that a new order was indeed coming. Complementing the negation of social distinctions that accompanied the conversion process was the assurance of salvation; this was the major theme of spiritual choruses. The spiritual choruses sung at camp meetings were in all respects "people's songs." They came from folk hymns of eighteenth-century New England Baptists, simple songs suited to group singing. They were redundant and brief, limited to those matters about which the community was in substantial agreement. The songs were disseminated through oral tradition, but they were also written down. As group statements, created by the plain folk and sung by all participants, the songs "may well have represented the common denominator of plain-folk religious belief."[10]

People's Songs explicitly acknowledged the religious roots of songs based on camp-meeting hymns and Negro spirituals. Hymns and spirituals were sung in their original forms as "people's songs" of peace and brotherhood. They also served as "zipper" songs; in a simple folk tune, built on repeated lines, the singer could "zip" on a word or phrase to make a new song. In this way, for example, in the song "We Shall Not Be Moved,"

"Jesus is my captain" had become "The union is our leader." These rhythmic, repetitive songs were easy to learn. They could get people singing together and creating their own songs.[11]

The parallels between camp-meeting and hootenanny songs go beyond their form to the meaning and effect of singing them. Songs may also have represented the "common denominator" of American Communist beliefs. The accessibility of songs, and of the particular form and content of "people's songs," helps explain their importance in holding the movement together. Songs expressed ideas simply; the audience could grasp the essence of an issue, in musical and poetic form, without having to understand an ideology or a sectarian language. "Talking Union" and "Song of My Hands," for example, illustrate the common denominator of the Left's view of labor in the 1940s.

There were of course sharp differences between a camp meeting and a hootenanny. People's Songsters' beliefs were expressed in political, rather than religious, terms. They believed in political action, since clearly faith alone would not create a socialist society. Still, the sense of dedication and solidarity expressed in the singing at a hoot was analogous—at times, consciously so—to the emotions revealed at a camp meeting. Lee Hays expressed the feeling aroused by singing hymns and the wish that labor songs could be sung with the same feeling: "What mattered was that we were singing. It was a drawing together of inner strengths, and what mattered was that each offered his voice to the others, and his own strength."[12]

The adaptation of a camp meeting made by late-nineteenth-century Populists and early-twentieth-century Socialists is even more analogous to the hootenanny because of its explicit political purpose. The "encampment," as it was called, proved to be the best way to reach poor people in isolated areas. In the early 1900s, organized Socialist encampments attracted as many as ten thousand people at one time to a collective meeting place where they could socialize with each other, listen to speeches by Eugene Debs and other popular orators, sing socialist songs, attend "educationals," and buy books and newspaper subscriptions. The encampment successfully blended entertainment with political education.[13]

Like Socialist encampments, Communist-oriented hootenannies expressed the values of the Left in form and substance.

Each served its respective movement by (1) combining folk and democratic traditions with socialist ideas; (2) providing the setting for a collective, unifying experience that contrasted with the isolation of daily life; (3) inspiring people by drawing on historical figures, events, and traditions, encouraging current efforts, and offering assurances of a radically different future. An encampment blended oratorical appeals to revolutionary traditions—represented by Jesus the Agitator, Tom Paine, Thomas Jefferson, and others from the socialist point of view—with the singing of hymns and socialist songs, often of populist origin. A hootenanny might differ in its specific political references. For example, the danger of the atom bomb or a tribute to Joe Hill might be a major theme, while direct religious references would be absent. Yet the appeals to the revolutionary American past were similar, as were the visions of a classless society. Similar as well were the unifying and inspirational effects of group singing. Some of the songs themselves, such as "The Farmer Is the Man," were the same.

If songs could bring about greater unity between people and convince them that they could collectively create their own future, the hootenanny seemed the ideal setting in which to effect these changes. Yet People's Songsters faced difficult problems communicating with their desired audience—problems that encampment organizers did not confront. Whereas the most successful Socialist encampment orators (those in the old Southwest) shared a common background, idiom, and culture with their audience, many People's Songs writers and performers lacked this common starting point. People's Songs hoped to reach an urban working-class audience of varied ethnic backgrounds, with rural (Appalachian) folk tunes as settings for topical songs. But due to the migration of rural whites and blacks into the cities during World War II, audiences themselves had changed. Urban audiences faced less physical isolation and more choices in terms of entertainment than had rural encampment audiences at the turn of the century; therefore, the hootenanny was unlikely to have the same significance in the lives of urban people as the encampment had had for rural people. Also, no matter what their ethnic or geographical backgrounds, people were becoming accustomed to having music performed for them by professionals, on radio and records, rather than making it themselves. Thus the new city-dwellers were less interested in traditional folk music than in commercial forms of country and blues music.[14]

People's Songs' inability to attract a larger following was not, however, primarily a question of the musical preferences of potential audiences. The popularity and influence of folk songs and folksingers did begin to spread in the 1940s. This was due in part to the work of professional musicians, such as Pete Seeger, who changed the singing style, harmonization, and accompaniment of traditional folk music, creating a sound more pleasing to urban audiences than that of traditional folk singers. At the same time, changes in the music industry made more types of music accessible to more people; many songs with local or regional popularity gradually entered the national consciousness. Urban audiences may have found the music and the substance of the songs a refreshing change of pace from popular songs of the time. Yet people's songs, and the tradition of protest singing, remained outside the realm of popular culture. Serge Denisoff claims this was due to the narrow ideological outlook—the "folk consciousness"—of left-wing writers and singers. This explanation may be broadened to say that the impact of People's Songs was limited, not primarily by geographical context or musical preference, but rather by insurmountable political obstacles.[15]

Domestic anticommunism subjected both to the organization and individual members to media attacks, blacklists, government spying, and other forms of intimidation. In 1948 police in Montreal, Quebec, confiscated copies of *The People's Song Book* from local bookstores. Following the Henry Wallace campaign, the Brooklyn College chapter of People's Songs was disbarred from campus by the college administration.

As early as 1946 articles attacking the group as a Communist front appeared in the New York *World-Telegram*, *Sun*, and other publications. The House Committee on Un-American Activities heard testimony about People's Songs in July 1947. *Counterattack*, a newsletter published by professional anti-Communists, included People's Songs among its list of "Party-line organizations" in September 1947. Over the next three years, *Counterattack* cited People's Songs as a "subversive organization" and a Communist front several times. A single article that claimed to document charges against a number of folksingers included attacks on most of the leaders of People's Songs. Earl Robinson says he stopped receiving calls from schools and unions after a *Time* magazine article in the late 1940s accused him of "crooning close to the party line." In 1949 the Tenney Committee of California cited People's Songs as a "vital Communist front," especially important to Communist propaganda work "because of its emphasis on appeal to youth and because of its organization and technique to provide entertainment for organizations and groups as a smooth opening wedge for Marxist-Leninist-Stalinist propaganda."[16]

Political attacks from without, combined with the Communist movement's postwar orthodoxy, made it impossible for People's Songs to maintain its valued ties with the labor movement. The CPUSA leadership had never shared People's Songs' belief in song as a weapon to change the world. The one group that did appear to share People's Songs' faith in the efficacy of song as a weapon was the FBI, which has in its files issues of the *Bulletin*, reports on People's Songs' national convention, logs of telephone conversations, names of activists, descriptions of leaflets, and more.[17] In short, People's Songs' connection to the Communist movement, despite the lack of organizational ties, was strong enough to cause the group all kinds of trouble with its potential allies and with the government without affording it a concomitant measure of support.

Even if the CP had offered more in the way of financial and moral support, it is questionable whether People's Songs' impact would have increased dramatically. The fact remains that the American Communist movement had no mass base of support. There was concern in the postwar period about high prices, housing shortages, Jim Crow, and the atom bomb. People's Songsters insisted on singing about these issues even after it became clear that to do so would lead to being attacked as "un-American." Yet one would be hard pressed to argue that People's Songsters articulated the aspirations of the American working class. A case can be made, by contrast, that popular Socialist encampment speakers in the early 1900s functioned as "organic intellectuals." Kate O'Hare, Oscar Ameringer, and Tom Hickey expressed the desires of, and provided leadership for, a particular class—small farmers and industrial workers in the old Southwest.[18] Communists in the 1940s, however, faced decreasing opportunities and abilities to speak for, or to, anyone but themselves.

A hootenanny was supposedly a great place to recruit others to the Communist movement. It was one of the few events to which Communists could bring people to introduce them to left-wing issues and concerns, and People's Songs had high hopes that the hootenanny would enable them to reach a broader audience. There were undoubtedly people who were affected by the musical and political excitement of hootenannies. In retrospect, however, recruiting was clearly much less significant than inspiring and encouraging those who were already committed to left-wing causes. As in other areas, Communists ended up singing and talking to each other.

Particularly during a time when the movement was in crisis, the singing at a hootenanny offered important emotional support. As People's Songs emphasized, songs differed from speeches: "Today, with the attacks on democracy here in America becoming more intense with each day's headlines, the need for our songs is greater than ever. We all know that a song can reach the minds and hearts of many people who will not listen to speeches or read tracts."[19] Group singing gave certification to people that there were alternatives to sitting in silence and that others shared their concerns. Irwin Silber, who served as People's Songs executive secretary, claims that songs build the "ideological cement" of a movement, "something that goes beyond the immediate political unity in the sense that you then get an emotional-ideological core of response, of feeling. . . . You can't build a movement just on that—it has to be rooted in politics—but politics alone will not cement that movement."[20] Others agree that the shared beliefs expressed in songs, and the process of singing them together, created and reinforced a sense of identity and unity which might otherwise have been lacking. Even political organizers who were not cultural workers themselves felt that songs were the single most important cultural aspect of the movement because of the unity they provided.[21]

Beyond its appeal to left-wing audiences and its role in supporting the movement, the hootenanny had particular significance to the performers themselves. Mario Casetta says that songs played a great role within the movement: "The singers themselves got tremendous sustenance, strength and morale out of the songs. How many of the opposition were reached is another matter." Ernie Lieberman explains how much he learned from interacting with other performers: "From Pete [Seeger]—enthusiasm, informality and song leading; from Laura Duncan (a black singer of spirituals, blues and show songs)—intensity, passion, conviction and a 'feel' for black music; from Betty Sanders—charm and precise delivery and the uses of songs in different languages." As Jerry Silverman expresses it, the hootenanny provided an opportunity for performers to develop their styles and test themselves. The hootenanny, he says, was "like being bathed in a great wave of love and enthusiasm."[22]

The hootenanny demonstrated the ways in which People's Songs' problems and accomplishments were connected because of its roots in the Communist movement. The main effect of People's Songs hootenannies was "to reinforce the feelings of the people on the Left, that what they were doing was right . . . and that they would win."[23] These gatherings thus reaffirmed the commitment of the Left while deepening its isolation, at least in the short term. The singing at a hootenanny was clearly an effective internal "weapon," helping to build and maintain the collective self-confidence necessary to challenge the dominant culture. But it is less clear what impact hootenannies may have had on the uninitiated. Earl Robinson claimed that the singing at a hootenanny created "an uplifting effect that would persist."[24] While people might have left these gatherings singing and feeling uplifted, there is no proof that such reactions were evidence of a change in consciousness or a heightened commitment to political activism. If songs were effective as weapons, it was unlikely that their impact would be so sudden and direct. This problem became more apparent during the Henry Wallace campaign, in which song as a weapon faced a severe challenge.

7

"The Fight for Peace": People's Songs and the Wallace Campaign

> I believe that peace . . . is the basic issue, both in the Congressional campaign this fall and right on through the Presidential election in 1948.
>
> How we meet this issue will determine whether we live, not in "one world" or "two worlds"—but whether we live at all.[1]

The kind of peace outlined by Henry Wallace in his September 12, 1946, speech in Madison Square Garden, based on cooperation and coexistence with the Russians, led President Truman to ask for Wallace's resignation from the Cabinet. Wallace resigned his position as secretary of commerce, promising to carry on the "fight for peace." As the last New Dealer left the government, currents developed which would in time lead to the creation of a third party.[2]

Wallace's philosophy of "progressive capitalism" was based on the New Deal heritage of concern for the common person combined with a strong defense of civil rights and the right to dissent. The key issue of the 1948 campaign, however, became the question of U.S.-Soviet relations. It was on the issue of communism that liberals who had formerly viewed Henry Wallace as Roosevelt's rightful heir opposed him in the 1948 campaign. Wallace's position ran counter to major statements of postwar American foreign policy. For example, in place of Henry Luce's "American century," in which U.S. power and ideals would be imposed on the world, Wallace posited the "century of the common man." In his Madison Square Garden speech, Wallace explicitly rejected the "get tough with Russia" policy, claiming that "the tougher we get, the tougher the Russians will get." His optimistic vision was summed up in a letter to Stalin, printed in the *New York Times* in May 1948: "There is no misunderstanding or difficulty between the United States of America and the Union of Soviet Socialist Republics which can be settled by force or fear and there is no difference which cannot be settled by peaceful, hopeful negotiation. There is no American principle or public interest, and there is no Russian principle or public interest which would have to be sacrificed to end the cold war and open up the Century of Peace which the Century of the Common Man demands."[3]

The Progressive party's "fight for peace" was doomed in the context of mounting cold-war tensions. Yet the Truman Doctrine and the Marshall Plan, combined with the domestic attack on civil liberties, convinced Henry Wallace and others that a third party was necessary if the people were to be given a choice—an opportunity to vote for peace—in the 1948 elections.[4] Despite a tremendous effort, the Progressive party made a dismal showing in the election. Wallace received 1,157,063 votes, 2.37 percent of the national vote, almost half of which came from New York. But the political and cultural significance of the Wallace campaign goes beyond the vote totals. As one historian expresses it, the Progressives "faced the real questions confronting postwar America."[5]

From its inception the Progressive party vastly overrated its potential. Even before the election the Progressive party claimed to have fought against Jim Crow, encouraged the will to peace all around the world, defeated universal military training and the Mundt-Nixon Bill (aimed at denying civil liberties to CP members and "Communist front" organizations), protected freedom of speech, delayed the cold war, and more.[6] But support from American labor and farm groups was hard to come by in the context of relative economic prosperity, high employment, and high farm prices. Wallace's claim to the Roosevelt heritage was preempted by Truman's shift to the left on domestic issues. Truman's "Fair Deal," veto of the Taft-Hartley Act, and attacks on the Republican-controlled Eightieth Congress helped people to forget his role in dismantling price controls in

1946 and his threats to draft striking railroad workers in 1947. The Democrats' vocal attack on racial discrimination also detracted from support of the third party.

More important than any of these measures in explaining the Progressive party's isolation and defeat was the larger crisis in American culture, expressed in terms of cold-war anticommunism. Postwar reaction and hysteria led to an acceptance of the doctrine of containment of the Soviet Union and to a demand for conformity. The Progressive party was formed on the basis of foreign policy in a political climate which was far from sympathetic to Wallace's internationalist crusade. Events in Europe in 1948 hurt the party as well. The Czechoslovakian coup and the Berlin blockade undermined the Progressives' claims of the possibilities for cooperating with the Soviet Union.

The Progressive party was repeatedly accused of being created and manipulated by the Communists—accusations that had extremely damaging effects. Indeed, some historians have concluded that the public perception of the Progressive party as Communist-dominated had more influence on the party than the CP itself. The Progressive party was subjected to harassment and intimidation throughout the campaign, making it clear that the major parties were alarmed. The Democrats welcomed the opportunity to present the Progressive party as Communist-controlled, thereby removing any possible stigma from themselves. The press played a crucial role in fostering this impression. The *Pittsburgh Press*, for example, published the names and addresses of those who had signed a petition to put Wallace on the ballot. Accompanying the list was a suggestion that people could clear their reputations by retracting their signatures.[7] Though it cost them votes and support, the Progressives remained true to their principles, refusing to repudiate Communist support that was in the interests of peace. They rejected as "un-American" the Red-baiting and attacks on civil liberties promoted by the major parties.

Contrary to its opponents' accusation, the Progressive party was not a creation of the CPUSA. The proposition of a third party had been discussed by CP leaders throughout 1946, but because of doubts about sufficient labor support they were still moving cautiously in mid-1947. As late as September, CP national secretary Eugene Dennis declared in a speech at Madison

Square Garden: "We Communists are not adventurers and irresponsible sectarians. We are not going to isolate ourselves. We never did and do not now favor the launching of premature and unrepresentative third parties or independent tickets."[8]

Only a month later the Cominform issued its manifesto calling for all Communist parties to place themselves in the vanguard of the opposition to American imperialism. CPUSA leaders interpreted this as a call to support a third party. By February of 1948 Eugene Dennis was apologizing for the CPUSA's slowness in recognizing the necessity of a third-party venture: "We were much too slow in combatting the erroneous views of certain party leaders and district organizations, as well as many of our trade union cadres who, up to the announcement of Wallace's candidacy, expressed doubts as to the advisability of an independent Presidential ticket."[9]

The Communists urged Wallace to run for the presidency and served as the most steadfast troops in "Gideon's Army." Yet it was not Communist pressure that convinced Wallace to run. According to John Morton Blum, "Believing that Truman was leading the country and the world toward war, committed to the contrary view of the new century, Wallace disregarded the warnings of his family and old friends and followed his own compulsion to stand political witness to his faith."[10] Wallace's running mate, Senator Glen H. Taylor of Idaho, summed up his and Wallace's position on the Communist issue in a nationwide radio address: "I am happy to have the support of all those who go along with our program. But just let me say to the Communists so there will be no misunderstanding, my efforts in the future as in the past will be directed toward the goal of making our economy work so well and our way of life so attractive and our people so contented that communism will never interest more than an infinitesimal fraction of our citizens who adhere to it now."[11]

Early successes raised the Progressive party's hopes of making a significant showing in the 1948 election and becoming an influence in national politics. The Progressives did not have a major problem raising money, as huge crowds paid to hear Wallace speak, and a number of wealthy supporters contributed to the campaign. By election day, Wallace supporters had managed to get him on the ballot in forty-four states. In California,

Progressives had gathered 464,000 signatures to get Wallace on the ballot. In a special congressional election in the Bronx, New York, saw Leo Isaacson, the American Labor candidate supported by Wallace, soundly defeated the Democratic candidate, Karl Propper. All of this created something of a political sensation, convincing the leaders of the Progressive party that they were a genuine people's party.

The CP leadership's expectations matched those of the Progressive party leadership, as illustrated in George Charney's reminiscence: "In the early part of 1948, the Progressive party seemed like a historic fulfillment, an independent Farmer-Labor party, the authentic American form of the People's Front that would unite the majority against imperialism and war and serve as the transitional stage in the march toward socialism."[12] Looking back on the 1948 elections, the CPUSA concluded that it had misunderstood the nature of the Progressive party: "There existed the wrong estimate that the formation of the Progressive party represented more than the simple emergence of an important fighting force for peace; that it represented in fact the emergence of a great mass People's party."[13] At the time, however, the CP welcomed Wallace's declaration of his independent candidacy: "We are voting peace and security for ourselves and our children's children. We are fighting for old-fashioned Americanism at the polls in 1948. We are fighting for freedom of speech and freedom of assembly. We are fighting to end racial discrimination. We are fighting for lower prices. We are fighting for free labor unions, for jobs, and for homes in which we can decently live."[14] Rank-and-file Communists and Progressives shared these high expectations, believing that the Wallace campaign signaled the beginning of a mass people's movement. The Progressive party also accorded songs a central place in the campaign, creating the most dramatic alliance of folk music and electoral politics in American history. In a list of reasons to vote for Wallace, poet Louis Untermeyer included this: "I will vote for Wallace since the Progressive Party is the only one which recognizes culture as a potentially powerful spirit in the life of the people."[15]

People's Songsters were among those who expected Wallace to poll five million votes. Their participation and efforts were as great as those of any rank-and-file Progressives; their failures were those of the Progressive party as well. Karl Schmidt's summation of the Progressives' experience also applies to People's Songsters' role in the campaign: "The story of their 'fight for peace' became a story of alternate hope and disappointment, coupled with an engulfing tide of events far beyond their control—or even their comprehension at the time."[16]

The Wallace campaign provided a test of People's Songsters' unique blend of Popular Front politics with folk song as a weapon. If their efforts are judged in terms of electoral votes, they were a complete failure. People's Songsters who expected the impact of their songs and singing to be direct and immediate were seriously mistaken. Songs probably did not convince anyone to vote for Wallace, just as the singing at hootenannies probably converted very few people to another world view. Nevertheless, the songs had short-term and long-term effects that deserve attention.

While maintaining structural independence from the Progressive party, People's Songs devoted the bulk of its resources to the 1948 campaign. The Progressive party gave money to People's Songs, half of which paid the salary of "Boots" Casetta, who maintained the music desk at party headquarters. Alan Lomax was in charge of music arrangements for the campaign. People's Songs screened hundreds of songs and produced and distributed songbooks, songsheets, and records. The organization also provided singers at meetings and made arrangements for musicians to go on campaign tours around the country. In Cleveland, in the absence of other strongly organized professional or business groups, the People's Songs chapter served as an organizing base for the Progressive party. Wallace himself wrote an article praising the singers and songs of the Progressive party.[17]

For People's Songs and the Communist movement, the Wallace campaign meant great work followed by great isolation. The campaign finalized the split between the CPUSA and the CIO; the CPUSA declined in numbers and influence, while the CIO continued its conservatizing trend.[18] In contrast to the fate of the Communist party, the movement culture maintained a certain strength due in part to the very drama, intensity, and desperation of the campaign. The songs and singers symbolize the strength demonstrated by the movement culture in the face of an impossible task. As in the case of the hootenanny, the most important effect of the songs was internal in the short run. Songs did not recreate the Popular Front, nor did they succeed as weapons to convince people to vote Progressive. Songs did, however, play a critical unifying and morale-building role within the Progressive campaign.

The extent of the Wallace campaign's failure was matched by the enthusiasm of the cultural workers who supported Wallace. Fred Hellerman says Wallace tapped the energy, hopes, and concerns of the postwar period. Many People's Songsters share Hellerman's memory of the campaign: "We went into it with tremendous energy. People worked their asses off. . . . I was sleepy all the time, out there singing six times a day, really punchy . . . running up to Harlem and singing on soundtrucks there, running down to Brooklyn, running out to Philadelphia to the convention . . . a very hectic, marvelous time." Hellerman says that, despite the low vote and people being afraid, working on the campaign was very rewarding as people discovered their own resources and found they could give voice to their concerns. People's Songsters were excited by the importance and recognition of their organization and their songs. As David Sear expresses it: "People's Songs made a tremendous effort and it was very exciting to be part of it . . . there were songs at every function." Ernie Lieberman says the campaign was "singing all the way . . . singing galore. . . . It goes to show how little it mattered in terms of votes. It mattered a great deal in terms of enthusiasm. It was wonderful." People's Songsters felt that their music and ideas were being heard, legitimated by Wallace and the campaign. The music was finally used "the way it was supposed to be used." Mario Casetta says the songs played a fantastic role as part of the day-to-day work of the campaign. "I don't think ever before and certainly not since has music been used in such an intelligent, creative, exciting way as it was during the Progressive party [campaign]."[19]

Songs were an integral part of the Wallace campaign. Sound trucks and caravans featured shows and music, and mass singing was part of every function. The Wallace campaign was often compared to a religious revival, and singing played a large part in creating such an impression. The Progressive party and People's Songs shared a belief in the power of song. They also shared a sense of urgency about reaching the people with their message of "Peace, Freedom and Abundance." These beliefs were expressed in *Songs for Wallace:* "Songs can move mountains, believe it or not; they can make people laugh or cry; and more important, they can help us fight. The songs given here, by describing the issues of today in simple human terms, can be great weapons in our fight to save America. Let us put these tunes on the lips of millions of citizens!"[20]

People's Songs approached its role in the Wallace campaign with characteristic zeal. The group's faith in the power of song was reaffirmed at the nominating convention, in retrospect the high point of the campaign's strength. Youth, enthusiasm, and rank-and-file participation characterized the Progressive party convention. As *Variety* reported, "No little part of the convention spirit stemmed from a campaign [song] notebook."[21] Observers noted the participation of delegates and visitors in singing the convention songs. CBS played recordings of convention singing, with commentary, on a nationwide program.

Laura Duncan, Michael Loring, Paul Robeson, Pete Seeger, and Jenny Wells, among others, established the central role of People's Songsters in the campaign by leading songs at the convention and the rally which followed. (More than thirty thousand people paid admission to attend the latter.) From then on, rallies and meetings began and ended with songs. Traveling with Wallace, Paul Robeson drew tremendous crowds. Pete Seeger accompanied Wallace on his courageous tour of the South, where the Progressives defied Jim Crow by refusing to hold segregated meetings. However, the power of song could not defuse southerners' violent reactions to the Progressive party. Such scenes as Pete Seeger challenging an angry southerner to sing "Dixie" with him, or an outraged Wallace demanding that southerners throwing eggs and tomatoes tell him if he was in America, did not seem humorous at the time.[22] One People's Songster summed up both the excitement and difficulty of the campaign: "The Wallace campaign was inspiring. I learned about Robeson and Pete and agreed with so much of what Wallace had to say. I was young and confused at the negative reaction that Wallace was receiving. 'Redbaiting' was hysterical in those days and clouded the issues. It was impossible to find anyone [with whom] to have an intelligent discussion about the campaign who wasn't already committed to Wallace, people were just so afraid."[23]

The Wallace campaign singing provides another example of how the very strength of the movement culture contributed to its isolation. Despite the enthusiasm with which songs were sung at meetings and rallies, and the fact that folk music began to reach a broader audience, the content of the songs was not taken to heart by "the people." One People's Songster explained frankly that the strength and enthusiasm of the campaign singing was also a weakness: "When you're singing very loudly, having a good time, it's a self-infecting kind of thing, and you imagine everybody else is also singing just as loudly and having just as good a time. *It's hard to hear all the people not singing* (emphasis added).[24]

Woody Guthrie's critique of the Progressive party campaign songs illustrates People's Songs' expectations that songs would have a direct impact on people's ideas and actions. In an essay called "My Ideas about the Use of People's Songs in the Progressive Party Movement to Elect Henry Wallace and Glen Taylor," Guthrie bluntly stated that the songs had failed to live up to their potential power as weapons:

> How much of the Progressive Party blowup and letdown is due to the failure of our songs? I say that the songs stood at the head of the list in attracting (for close inspection) some of the largest audiences ever ganged together to listen to the words, facts, prophecies, and freedom words of our artists and of our candidates; our songs, then, must surely stand up *first* to be counted, first to be taken apart nut by nut and bolt by bolt, first to be looked at under the most critical microscope that we can find to use.
>
> Why did our songs not reach in and touch deep enough to cause the hand to push the C Row handles in that voting booth?[25]

Guthrie's remarks also reveal some of the aesthetic and political problems faced by People's Songs. He expressed serious reservations about the quality of songs which "we people's song-spinners turned out to make the average voter know and love the several million good things which our Progressive Party had to offer. . . . A dozen things were wrong with our songs and in the ways we used them." Guthrie's criticism was aimed at campaign songs such as "I've Got A Ballot," which he described as "a shallow, jingly and insincere number. . . . People I have seen call their vote a number of things, none of which are nearly as cutie-pie, as highly polite, as flippant . . . as this song."[26] "I've Got A Ballot" appeared in *Songs for Wallace* with this introduction: "This parody on 'I've Got Six-Pence' was easily one of the favorites at the Progressive Party Convention. After you sing at a meeting or party, chances are that this will be one of the songs people will be singing as they leave."

I've Got A Ballot

I've got a ballot,
A magic little ballot,
I've got a ballot,
And it means my life.

It can bring a higher wage,
It can pension my old age,
It can make a little home for kids and wife.

The Republicans they grieve me,
The Democrats only deceive me,
I've a brand new party, believe me,
As we go rolling up the vote.

Roll it up for Wallace!
Roll it up for Taylor!
There is magic in that ballot
when you vo-o-o-o-te!

Happy is the day
When the people get their way,
As we go rolling up the vote.[27]

Other People's Songsters share, at least in retrospect, Guthrie's contempt for some of the campaign songs; Pete Seeger says People's Songs could have knocked people off their feet with better songs. But Guthrie's political critique was more problematic. He claimed that "the people are lots more ready than our songs and our songleaders are ready to admit . . . we are not allowing our songs to be radical enough in the proper ways." Guthrie had few alternatives to offer, however. His own songs for Wallace were far from his best work. His essay failed to explain how printing "Passing Through" or holding

"Cowboy-Hillbilly-Religious" brands of hootenannies, as he recommended, added up to being "radical enough in the proper ways."[28]

Woody Guthrie's critique of Progressive party songs is significant. His complaints reflect the cultural theory he shared with People's Songsters, which was neither an art-for-art's-sake position nor a demand that art be sacrificed for ideological purity. Guthrie and other People's Songsters were uncomfortable with the "pop" sound of some of the campaign songs, believing that the folk idiom was the best means of reaching more people with a serious political message. Guthrie's critique is a revealing example of the contradictions inherent in People's Songsters' outlook. On the one hand, they sincerely desired to take a broad approach musically and politically, to listen as well as talk to "the people." On the other hand, they assumed that folk songs were obviously superior and that the people were "ready" to hear and act upon their message. Such assumptions only increased the isolation already imposed by the political climate. It is doubtful that more serious political songs would have had more impact on voters or made People's Songs able to hear "all the people not singing."

The Wallace campaign songs most likely had no effect at all on those who were undecided about how to cast their vote. Truman's move to the left on domestic issues, the Red-baiting of the Progressive party, and events in Europe were all more decisive factors. Yet, despite criticism of their uneven quality, the songs did boost the morale of the third party's supporters. The writers of "Put It on the Ground," a People's Songs' favorite, were responsible for the Progressive party convention favorite, "The Same Merry-Go-Round":

The donkey is tired and thin
The elephant thinks he'll move in
They yell and they fuss,
But they ain't foolin' us
'Cause they're brothers right under the skin.

It's the same, same merry-go-round
Which one will you ride this year?
The donkey and elephant bob up and down
On the same merry-go-round.[29]

Campaign songs are rarely durable, and the Progressive party songs proved no exception. Like many other people's songs, the campaign songs disappeared after fulfilling their function. The more lasting cultural impact of the campaign came from the exposure and growing popularity of folk and topical songs. People's Songsters saw the Wallace campaign as a turning point in American popular music. Many good songs were used—songs that were different than those written just for the campaign. Woody Guthrie's "Roll on Columbia" is one example, say former People's Songsters, of a song with good music and lyrics that would be used again and again. People were moved by the songs, including "reporters who saw the campaign as Communist-run, Wallace as a fool and a dupe, but the music thrilled them. It didn't change their view but prepared them for an acceptance of a whole new mode of expression, where it was right to use social criticism in song, right to deal with profound and important subjects in song (not just 'I love you, you love me')." Another participant says: "We all did what we could to use these songs in support of Wallace, at political meetings and everywhere we could. I think it played as big a role as it could in the Wallace campaign. And the singers were identified with the campaign, and part of the love of these singers today goes back to their participation in the Wallace campaign." While the campaign may have been foredoomed, the seed was planted that led to bigger and better things.[30]

With hindsight, cultural workers seem to view the campaign differently than some of the more strictly political activists. People's Songsters who claim that their efforts on behalf of the Wallace campaign were doomed because of the cold war say they would do it over again. They are still convinced, as they were then, of the righteousness of their cause and the necessity of speaking out against the "cold war madness." By contrast, the more political Communists tend to view the campaign in retrospect as a mistake. The third-party effort, they claim, was the basis for the CP's isolation from the labor movement and one of the main reasons the attack on the Left took place. Art Shields concludes that "it was probably a mistake to have founded the Third Party—conditions weren't right for it and it absorbed a tremendous amount of energy."[31]

The enthusiasm of People's Songsters undoubtedly caused them to overestimate their impact at the time. Although in August of 1948, L. Haize (Lee Hays) reported that "in short, what should be said now is that a people's culture came into its own,"[32] neither a people's culture nor a third party with any future prospects came into its own in 1948. The Wallace campaign was the end of the line for some People's Songsters. Burl Ives, Tom Glazer, Josh White, and Oscar Brand repudiated the Left, finding commercial success singing for politically safe audiences. People's Songs did not dissolve when the campaign ended, however. The editors of the *Bulletin*, among others, planned to continue their efforts unabated.

Where to? What Next?

> The American people need People's Songs more than ever before. . . . We will put singers to work. . . . We will master the techniques of mass singing. . . . We will hold hundreds of new hootenannies. . . . We will sing together. . . . We will set up distribution centers in every community.[33]

People's Songsters' determination and faith was reaffirmed in a new song, published in the November 1948 issue of the *Bulletin*. The song, "Wasn't That a Time!" called on the strength and inspiration of past freedom fighters to provide inspiration for the future. The song began this way:

> Our fathers bled at Valley Forge
> The snow was red with blood,
> Their faith was warm at Valley Forge,
> Their faith was brotherhood.
>
> Wasn't that a time!
> Wasn't that a time!
> A time to try the soul of man!
> Wasn't that a terrible time!

The song also reiterated People's Songsters' feeling that the time was a critical one for determining the future direction of American politics and culture. If people would join them, they could make a difference. The last verse and chorus said:

Our faith cries out . . . They shall not pass
We cry No Pasaran
We pledge our lives, our honor, all
To free . . . this prisoned land.

Isn't this a time!
Isn't this a time!
A time to free the soul of man!
Isn't this a wonderful time![34]

The song inadvertently illustrates People's Songs' dilemma. While bravely defiant, the song was only likely to have meaning to the Communist Left. The phrase "No Pasaran" from the Spanish Civil War demonstrated People's Songs connection to the Popular Front, but it was out of sync in the 1940s.[35]

Despite its plans and hopes for the future, People's Songs was forced to dissolve in March 1949 because of a lack of funds. A *Sunday Worker* article, printed the first week of March, praised the work of People's Songs, "a lusty baby of three," adding an ironic touch to the organization's sudden dissolution.[36] People's Songs was a victim of the cold war and its own blind faith in the inevitability of socialism. Yet in spite, and because, of the forces arrayed against them, some People's Songsters persisted in their fight to create a world in which a "people's culture" would flourish. The last issue of the *Bulletin* emphasized that the job begun by People's Songs was far from complete: "Obviously, the work begun by People's Songs will continue, for, more than ever, America needs the singers, musicians, and composers who have said that they know which side they are on. . . . The American people, along with the people of the rest of the world, have a fight on their hands for peace, democracy and security, and the members of People's Songs, we know, will be in the thick of this fight."[37]

These sentiments were soon expressed in a hopeful new song written by Pete Seeger and Lee Hays, "Tomorrow Is a Highway":

Tomorrow is a highway broad and fair,
And we are the many who'll travel there.
Tomorrow is a highway broad and fair,

And we are the workers who'll build it there;
And we will build it there.

Tomorrow is a highway broad and fair
And hate and greed shall never travel there
But only they who've learned the peaceful way
Of brotherhood, to greet the coming day;
We hail the coming day.©[38]

In July 1949 People's Artists was founded to take over the work of People's Songs. Pete Seeger and Irwin Silber were among those elected to the steering committee, and at the first meeting Paul Robeson spoke about the need for such a new music organization. The first concert sponsored by People's Artists brought immediate and unexpected publicity. Featuring Paul Robeson and others, the concert in Peekskill, New York, was broken up by local vigilantes. It was rescheduled, in defiance of what People's Artists perceived as incipient native fascism, and this time took place without incident. After the concert, however, mobs of people, uncontrolled by the police, stoned the cars of those who had attended the concert. More than 150 people were hospitalized as a result of the "Peekskill Riot."[39]

Peekskill became a symbol for both the hardening of anti-communism and the Communists' desperate attempts to fight back. The latter were illustrated in the Weavers' recording of the Peekskill story, "Hold the Line":

Let me tell you the story of a line that was held
And many men and women whose courage we know well
As they held the line at Peekskill on that long September day
We will hold the line forever till the people have their way.[40]

Similar sentiments were reflected in Paul Robeson's defiant statement following the concert: "I shall take my voice wherever there are those who want to hear the melody of freedom or the words that might inspire hope and courage in the face of despair and fear. My weapons are peaceful for it is only by peace that peace can be attained. The song of Freedom must prevail."[41]

People's Artists made an important contribution to keeping folk and topical songs in public view during a difficult period. It produced hootenannies, provided performers for radical func-

The first cover of *Sing Out!* magazine, featuring "The Hammer Song" (© Sing Out Corporation, used by permission)

Sing Out! cover, July 1950 (© Sing Out Corporation, used by permission)

tions, began its own record company, published the major left-wing songbook of the McCarthy era, *Lift Every Voice,* and was involved in many programs associated with the arts in the Communist movement. The major themes addressed by People's Artists were the dominant themes of the Communist movement in the early 1950s: peace, civil liberties, and civil rights. People's Artists supported the Progressive party campaign in 1952, although on a more limited scale than People's Songs' 1948 effort. The organization made a major effort to save accused atomic spies Julius and Ethel Rosenberg in 1952 and 1953.

In May 1950 People's Artists began to publish a song magazine to succeed the *People's Songs Bulletin. Sing Out!* would become the major publication of the 1960s folk revival. Its title was taken from "The Hammer Song," written by Lee Hays and Pete Seeger, which served as the cover feature for the first issue. The song symbolized the defiance of those who remained committed to the Left:

> If I had a hammer, I'd hammer in the morning,
> I'd hammer in the evening—all over this land.
> I'd hammer out danger! I'd hammer out a warning!
> I'd hammer out love between all of my brothers—
> All over this land.©[42]

Despite the shared goals, activities, and personnel, People's Artists differed in significant ways from People's Songs. People's Artists was more overtly ideological and dogmatic than People's Songs had been. As their isolation grew, Communists and their allies worked harder to justify maintaining an unpopular ideological position. The songs were more doctrinaire and sectarian, reflecting the atmosphere on the Communist Left, and political standards tended to outweigh aesthetic concerns. Ernie Lieberman, who was an editor of *Sing Out!* for a year and a half, admits that he put in songs that were politically right even when he knew he wouldn't sing them. Pete Seeger and the Weavers distanced themselves from People's Artists' activities.[43]

In addition to being highly critical of Tin Pan Alley, People's Artists shared the Communist movement's concerns with "male chauvinism" and "white chauvinism" within the movement. These concerns were manifested in *Sing Out!*'s criticism of the Weavers—Pete Seeger, Lee Hays, Fred Hellerman, and Ronnie Gilbert—who had begun singing together at People's Songs hootenannies in 1948. The quartet was accused of catering to Tin Pan Alley female stereotypes, and in a more explosive debate, the Weavers were criticized for being an all-white group singing black songs. Fred Moore touched off the debate by saying that all-white groups could not "get across the content, intention and deep feeling of the songs precisely because they have no direct connection with Negroes in a performance capacity."[44] An open discussion entitled "Can an All-White Group Sing Songs from Negro Culture?" ran in subsequent issues.[45] Most of the published responses, including an editorial statement by the People's Artists executive board, agreed with Moore.

At the same time, *Sing Out!* and People's Artists paid attention to black history and music, promoted the careers of black artists, and criticized the commercial exploitation of black culture by the entertainment industry. For the most part, however, People's Artists' orientation was even more internal than People's Songs' had been. People's Artists functioned as a more direct cultural arm of the Communist movement due to the cold war, the weakness of the Communist Left, and limited financial resources. These problems led to the decision to disband People's Artists in the fall of 1956 and channel future efforts into the production of *Sing Out!* During the People's Artists' years, subscriptions to *Sing Out!* did not match those of the *People's Songs Bulletin.* In the fall of 1954, when *Sing Out!* shifted to quarterly publication and began to work toward a less polemical and more balanced tone, the magazine had one thousand subscribers.[46]

While People's Artists reached fewer people as the Communist Left disintegrated, the organization continued the legacy of People's Songs, including a focus on issues, on folk and topical songs, and on ways of sharing those songs. Again the hootenanny stands out as a significant aspect of this legacy. Similar to People's Songs, People's Artists received much of its income from hootenannies, which continued to play an important role on the Left in the 1950s. As Joseph Starobin expressed it at the time: "The Hootenanny is an institution by now. It answers the deep needs of our time, of solidarity. It does so in a language that makes sense to many millions whom progressives are not

Sing Out! cover, July 1951, featuring Paul Robeson (second from left) with the People's Artists Quartet (left to right): Ernie Lieberman, Laura Duncan, Osborne Smith, Betty Sanders (© Sing Out Corporation, used by permission)

at the moment reaching in other ways, the language of dance and song. The Hootenanny is not just something to enjoy, but something to think about."[47] In Irwin Silber's terms, 1950s hoots were one of the few visible expressions of the Left during the time of the worst repression. People's Artists ran a lot of hootenannies, which Silber says were especially important for reaching young people. They became an act of defiance, publicly associated with politics at a time when few left-wing groups ran activities in their own names. Though they could no longer get into good halls, they still had large and vital audiences.[48] Ironically, as domestic cold-war tensions reached their peak and the American Left disintegrated, folk music and folksingers worked their way into popular culture and consciousness. Folk music became more common in film, theater, radio, and nightclubs. It also began to be adapted into commercial popular songs. Hootenannies and folk music concerts and festivals continued to increase in popularity.[49] In the 1960s, hootenannies became the cultural vehicle through which folk music and the New Left intersected.

The most significant development in the growing popularity of folk music in the 1950s was the success of the Weavers. When the Weavers landed a job at the Village Vanguard in December 1949, they hoped to make enough money to enable them to stay together and sing. Their success was far beyond anyone's expectations, including their own. Soon after singing to large, enthusiastic crowds at the Village Vanguard, the Weavers found themselves with a hit record on their hands and offers from nightclubs all over the country. "Goodnight Irene" sold close to two million records; between 1950 and 1952, more than four million Weavers' records were sold. The Weavers' commercial career was cut short by the blacklist of left-wing entertainers, but their initial and striking success revealed the potential audience for a popular brand of folk music. The group was the most important forerunner of the folk revival of the 1960s.[50]

The Wallace campaign, like the hootenanny, carried on the musical and political traditions to which People's Songs was committed: popularizing folk music, educating people in song about current issues, getting people to participate in creating their own music and politics. The problems and accomplish-

The Weavers (photo by Sonia Handelman, used by permission. All rights reserved.)

ments of hootenannies and the Wallace campaign were similar. In spite of anti-Communist hysteria and successful blacklists in the 1950s, the songs, singers, and issues that had characterized People's Songs lived on. People's Songsters' sincere and courageous efforts to use folk song as a weapon were doomed in the short run. But the survival of a movement culture, of which the songs were an integral part, meant that the individual self-respect, collective self-confidence, and vision required to combat the dominant culture were in some ways passed on to the next generation concerned with similar issues. Folk song as a weapon reappeared in the 1960s, playing a significant role in building, and expressing the unity and determination of, a new movement culture.

8

"We Will Overcome": The Legacy of People's Songs

> There is no mistaking their sincerity, their deep and genuine concern for human misery. . . . And there is no mistaking the fact that they made a deliberate choice, at a critical point in their career, to state their political and social views in public concerts, whatever the damage to their professional career.
>
> They sang at prisons, at poorhouses, at the smallest church that asked for them. . . . They sang for the poor, the slaves, the freedmen, the Irish, women, Republicans, sailors. They were a voice crying out for freedom, peace, equality.[1]

With a few changes, Charles Hamm's comments on the Hutchinson family's career in the 1840s could be applied to People's Songsters' activity one hundred years later. Hamm claims tremendous accomplishments for the Hutchinsons: "It may well be that the Hutchinsons altered the course of American history, that their music hastened the confrontations and conflicts that led inexorably to the Civil War, that their songs fanned passions and created the sense of togetherness and resolve necessary to convert ideas and ideals into action, that their singing of 'John Brown's Body' converted more people to the antislavery cause than all the speeches and sermons of the time."[2] The impact of People's Songs cannot be stated so clearly. People's Songsters did not change the world with songs in a perceptible way in the postwar years. Songs did not function primarily as weapons to organize, unify, or raise the political consciousness of labor and the American people. Songs may have had such effects indirectly in the long run. In the short run, however, the impact of People's Songsters was felt primarily within the movement.

Their involvement with left-wing politics and folk music dramatically changed the lives of People's Songsters. Affected at an early age by the blend of left-wing and folk culture, they in turn tried to reach others in the same way. Jerry Silverman sums up the feelings of many former People's Songsters: "My involvement [with the Left], especially through music, changed the course of my life and I'm convinced it changed the course of American life, culturally."[3]

Irwin Silber claims that People's Songs was important for the internal life of the Left and for reaching out into broader arenas of American life. Earl Robinson and others agree that one important aspect of People's Songs' impact was helping people inside and outside the movement develop an appreciation for folk material. Many former People's Songsters echo Jackie Gibson Alper's assessment of their impact as "less than we thought it was at the time, but definitely more than current detractors of our movement now assess it to have been." Alper comments on both the internal and external effects: "Certainly we contributed to the rallying of numbers of working people, to their political education, somewhat, and to the buoying of spirits and reinforcing strengths in time of struggle. Certainly, too, the development of the entire U.S. folk-topical-pop song was directly influenced by the activities of People's Songs artists and the groups they gave birth to and those groups and individuals following them, right to the present time."[4]

People's Songs clearly had an impact on the Communist movement. Though songs could not save the movement from itself, nor from cold-war anticommunism, they could provide support and encouragement in a difficult time. People's songs and singers offered more than entertainment, reminding activists of the righteousness and urgency of the issues in which they were engaged. People's songs represented the common denominator of Communist beliefs and, sung collectively, served as one means of unifying people within a shared movement culture. Indirectly, People's Songs suggested that an alternative culture went hand in hand with an alternative politics. If the songs and singers were not notable for their ability to recruit others, their importance to the movement itself should not be underestimated.

Assessing the external effects of People's Songs is more difficult. People's Songs' work did not immediately change the world, but it did have some lasting effects on American culture. Hootenannies, concerts, records, and the Wallace campaign contributed to the popular exposure of folk performers such as Woody Guthrie, Huddie Ledbetter (Leadbelly), Josh White, and Pete Seeger. These talented artists helped people appreciate folk material more, while continuing a long tradition of protest singing. In the 1950s this tradition was expressed most significantly by the civil rights movement. One book of freedom songs (*We Shall Overcome!*) includes adaptations of the Wobbly song "They Go Wild over Me" and Florence Reece's "Which Side Are You On?" along with "The Hammer Song." The same work explains how "We Shall Overcome" became such an important song:

> This modern adaptation of the old Negro church song, "I'll Overcome Someday," has become the unofficial theme song for the freedom struggle in the South . . . . Negro Textile Union workers adapted the song for their use sometime in the early '40s and brought it to Highlander Folk School. It soon became the school's theme song and associated with Zilphia Horton's singing of it. She introduced it to union gatherings all across the South. On one of her trips to New York, Pete Seeger learned it from her and in the next few years he spread it across the North. Pete, Zilphia and others added verses appropriate to labor, peace and integration sentiments: We will end Jim Crow. . . . We shall live in Peace. . . . We shall organize. . . . The whole wide world around . . . etc.[5]

Rev. David A. Noebel, writing for Christian Crusade Publications on "the Communist use of music," tells the story this way: "The folksong, 'We Shall Overcome,' was introduced into the Communist-planned Negro revolution through the Highlander Folk School."[6] A participant in the civil rights movement comments on the song's power: "One cannot describe the vitality and emotion this one song evokes across the Southland. I have heard it sung in great mass meetings with a thousand voices singing as one; I've heard a half-dozen sing it softly behind the bars of the Hinds County Prison in Mississippi; I've heard old women singing it on the way to work in Albany, Georgia; I've heard the students singing it as they were being dragged away to jail. It generates power that is indescribable."[7] And Frank Hamilton explains it in terms of "people's songs": "Sometimes 'the people' can have the songs come back to them in a different way than they sang them to begin with. 'We Shall Overcome' was like that. The word 'overcome' took on new meaning when Guy Carawan sang it in North Carolina at the sit-ins."[8]

The work of People's Artists also contributed to sustaining what Simon Frith calls "an alternative way of music-making."[9] People's artists continued to insist on singing what they wanted and on confronting political issues in song, as illustrated in the challenge to McCarthyism in "In Contempt":

> Build high, build wide your prison wall
> That there be room enough for all
> Who hold you in contempt
> Build wide, til all the land be locked inside.[10]

Folk and topical songs continued to be used in protest movements throughout the 1950s and 1960s, but it was with the commercial success of the Weavers that, as Pete Seeger explains, "our particular brand of folk music began to reach a broader audience."[11]

Bert Spector has suggested that Pete Seeger's brand of folk music could have become popular sooner were it not for the political context. Seeger had a successful engagement at the Village Vanguard in the spring of 1947, as the Red-baiting attacks in the entertainment industry were beginning to mount. Spector also argues that there was not widespread public support for the blacklist of the Weavers in the early 1950s. Yet it is a mistake to conclude from this that the audience for Seeger and the Weavers was concerned only with music and not with politics. Audiences who came out to hear Seeger and the Weavers, or who attended hootenannies, in the 1950s were defying the hegemonic process. They actively defended their own freedoms while supporting the singers' right to be heard.[12]

The problem of separating the music from the politics is expressed in David Sear's comments about the Weavers: "They were so good musically . . . and so exciting, and said all the right things, and sang all the right things. And they did take over America as number one in the popular music field. If it wasn't for the politics, they would have gone on forever as the deans of American folk music. But . . . where would they have been if it wasn't for the politics?"[13]

Where would the Weavers have been without their politics? They met in the context of the movement culture, at summer camp and at left-wing political and cultural affairs in New York City. The four first sang together at a People's Songs' hootenanny. Without this common ground, they might not have developed a shared outlook toward music and politics. They certainly would not have conceived of the Weavers as being like the Almanacs—only "with discipline."[14] They might not have known the same songs, especially those they valued because of their origins, among them Woody Guthrie's and Leadbelly's songs, which they popularized. Were it not for their specific politics, they might not have had the broad view of folk music which allowed them to rewrite and rearrange songs in order to reach a broader audience. And they might not have had the commitment to persist in hard times, believing their songs would have an effect: "We felt that if we sang loud enough and strong enough and hopefully enough, somehow it would make a difference."[15]

The Weavers' singing did "make a difference." They continued a process to which People's Songs had been devoted—bringing folk-style music into public view, interpreting it, defining it broadly, and making it accessible to masses of people. The popular music industry began to spread the Left's broad view of folk music. The Weavers' unique style was described as "a rejection of surface 'authenticity' to arrive at a deeper authenticity."[16] They rewrote and rearranged songs in order to sing them with the spirit and enthusiasm that captivated both audiences and critics. There was a serious core to their joking introduction, "Now we are going to sing an old folk song that we wrote last week."[17] In short, the Weavers' success began to legitimize the writing and singing of folk-style songs with social and political content. The re-expression and creation of "folk songs" in a form in which people could digest them, linked with the content, laid the foundation for the folk boom of the 1960s.

People's songs and artists played an important role in building a new movement culture in the 1960s. The old songs provided a sense of history and continuity which the New Left, in its typically American style, was sorely lacking. The artists became symbols of the Old Left's courage and tenacity in defying the dominant culture against great odds. Some of the aesthetic concerns—such as the emphasis on issues rather than technique—and the optimism of the old folk movement carried on, at least for a while. According to Simon Frith, young white political activists in the 1960s "found in folk music the only expressive form that could be made directly responsive to their political concerns, that could serve the same cultural purpose as black music did for its listeners."[18] The most successful 1960s artists viewed themselves as direct descendants of Old Left "people's artists." Bob Dylan fashioned himself after Woody Guthrie, while Peter, Paul, and Mary saw themselves as "the Weavers' children." During the 1960s folk revival, what became popular were not just topical and folk songs, but the more emotional-philosophical songs that People's Songsters point to as "good songs"—Bob Dylan's "Blowin' in the Wind," Paul Simon's "The Sounds of Silence," and Pete Seeger's adaptation of a poem from a Russian novel: "Where Have All the Flowers Gone?" Mario Casetta says: "One of the best anti-war songs in the world, in my opinion, is 'Where Have All the Flowers Gone?' and that doesn't say 'Ban Nuclear Bombs'—it doesn't have to."[19]

The current *nueva cancion* (new song) movement in Latin America is a revival (or survival) in some of the same ways as was the 1960s folk boom in the United States. *Canto nuevo* consists of both residual and emergent elements. It includes a variety of music, from traditional folk to pop and rock; the lyrics focus on a wide variety of themes. Though this is very much a youth movement, the old songs and artists play a critical role. For example, Victor Jara's songs and courage have not been forgotten, and a popular song in Chile plays on the slogan *El pueblo unido jamas sera vencido* (The people united will never be defeated) with the line "Tenderness united will never be conquered." The broad outlook of the new song movement is reminiscent of People's Songs. "Adherents define *canto nuevo* as an attitude toward life," reports the *New York Times*.[20] According to Ricardo Garcia, the record producer whose company produces the songs in Chile, "'It is essentially humanist.'"[21]

The growing popularity of songs celebrating democratic rights and the unity of the people indicates a new spirit and form of resistance. According to the *New York Times*, it is the music that has sparked the growing political protest in Chile.

Political activity has been banned since General Augusto Pinochet took power, after the democratically elected president, Salvador Allende, was overthrown in 1973. As the *Times* explains, "Young painters, poets and playwrights tested the limits of Government censorship, which bans anything the Government construes as political. But it is music that has the greatest impact because of its popular access . . . the stirring of young people and their music has grown . . . to become a driving force behind the current protests by Chileans demanding a return to democratic rule. The protests have shaken this country."[22] *Canto nuevo* has been met with repression, indicating that it threatens the dominant culture. The government has responded to the growing popularity of *canto nuevo* by prohibiting festivals of the music and limiting the amount of time it can be performed on television. At one point Ricardo Garcia was jailed for a week for releasing a song by an exiled singer. "But the music nonetheless continues to be heard increasingly," reports the *Times*.[23]

One pertinent question here concerns the connection between an alternative culture and a political movement. If the new song movement presents itself as essentially "humanist," what is the specific substance of its vision? This is similar to People's Songs' problems of emphasizing freedom and democracy, hoping to be popular and reach a broad spectrum of people, yet at the same time wanting to communicate a particular message based on socialist ideals. Could People's Songs have combined more effectively its populist approach and socialist vision? Can a movement culture ever overcome its isolation and learn to listen as well as talk to "the people"?

What if People's Songs had not been connected with the Communist movement? What if its approach to song as a weapon had been less naive and less sectarian? Such speculation assumes that we can easily separate the Communist Left's problematic politics from its cultural accomplishments: the politics can be rejected as bad; the culture, adopted as good. Yet of course the conclusion is not so simple; the political and cultural legacies of American Communism are inextricably linked. People's Songs existed in large part because of its commitment to Communism; its accomplishments and failures developed out of that commitment. On the one hand, their commitment to the movement limited the impact of People's Songsters. On the other hand, the same passionate commitment—based on genuine concern for helping people live better lives—inspired great creative effort and explains their positive contributions.

In some ways, then, an evaluation of the impact of People's Songs is linked to an assessment of the effects of American Communism. With hindsight, former People's Songsters offer incisive assessments of the Communist movement's strengths and weaknesses during the time of their participation. They are especially critical of their own sectarianism and unquestioning faith in the Soviet Union. Ronnie Gilbert says the American Left was not in touch with what was really happening. "There was a kind of optimism and hopefulness, which by the way I cherish because it's hard to come by today. . . . I don't feel cynical about it; I just feel that one has to find a different kind of source for it. It's as necessary to decent human life and the possibility of decent human life as water. . . . We were maybe too full of ourselves, too sectarian. As long as we hung out with each other, it looked as if everything was gonna go great. Here we were, all gung-ho for love and brotherhood and peace, and holding hands across the ocean. . . . I still believe it! I just don't think it resides in a political system alone."[24] Many People's Songsters mention the American Left's focus on the Soviet Union as a big problem—one that they would address if they had it to do over again. Asked what he would do differently, Pete Seeger says, "I wouldn't have the faith in Joseph Stalin I had in 1937. On the other hand, I'm glad I did not disassociate myself from the Left."[25]

Why would they do it over again, knowing their efforts were doomed to failure? They praise the Left for dedication, self-sacrifice, idealism, courage, solidarity, and leadership on important issues. They point to the Left's political and cultural contributions. David Sear, for example, mentions the valuable ideas and consciousness-raising efforts of the Left; he also mentions that "We Shall Overcome" showed how songs could be effective. Participants speak proudly, not apologetically, of People's Songs' work. Their comments reveal both the personal and political meaning of the period, the pride and the disappointment. Waldemar Hille refers to the People's Songs' years as "a glorious period in the cultural development of the U.S." Irwin Silber says, "We pretty well maximized the potential of that movement." Pete Seeger again expresses the feeling of many former People's Songsters about their work: "We did our best but it wasn't enough."[26]

In retrospect, People's Songsters are critical of their own work, claiming that they interpreted "art as a weapon" too narrowly. They would be likely to agree with Stanley Aronowitz's criticism of "the narrowly construed concept of political art," which requires the subordination of form to content, and content to political truths, as "antithetic to critical consciousness and to a revolutionary art."[27] Yet it is unlikely that People's Songs could have been more expansive without a different political orientation. In any case, many former People's Songsters continue to share the idea that cultural activity has an important effect on people's lives. As Jackie Gibson Alper expresses it: "Some were reached by our songs—perhaps not as many as I once thought—but more than we could have expected as they are *still* being reached both by our musical posterity and by some of us oldsters who are still carrying on in the belief that culture is and can be a force for progress for humankind."[28] Indeed, all the People's Songsters I interviewed have carried on in this belief, despite the extent of their political failure in the 1940s. They may have drifted away from the Communist movement in the 1950s, but their cultural efforts have continued to this day. Some still perform (music, dance, theater), some teach guitar or banjo, some write songs, edit or publish music or teaching manuals. Though few are involved with political organizations, their ideals have not changed dramatically. As Pete Seeger says, "The basic philosophy of socialism is still the only one that makes sense for the human race."[29]

Along with their continued commitment, however, comes a continuing ambivalence about commercial success and pop music. The fear of being corrupted by the commercial arena was expressed by Woody Guthrie during the People's Songs period: "We've got a good bunch of players and singers at People's Songs and around People's Artists. I'd rather to put out every word of mine through Leadbelly, Pete, Cisco, and the others in our own ways. We've got to break down this log jam, this taboo, this blacklist, this door of distribution that is locked against us, and if I sign over on the log jammers side I'd be used against everybody and everything we believe in."[30]

The ambivalence toward the popular music industry that had confounded People's Songs came to the surface of the folk movement when the Weavers became a commercial success. The Weavers were criticized by some for selling out. They were accused of destroying the integrity of the songs with the pop orchestral arrangements of their early recordings, of rewriting the lyrics of songs to dilute the political message, of not doing justice to Negro songs as an all-white group, and of avoiding singing at left-wing affairs to protect their commercial careers. Despite the criticism and reservations of some leftists, however, the reaction of many People's Songsters was great excitement: "Our guys had finally made it."[31] People who had worked for years in relative isolation were thrilled to hear songs they knew and loved pouring out of radios and record stores.

The question remains, however, what the songs mean to a broader audience in a different context. The fact that the Weavers worked through the mass media undeniably affected their music, especially in the early stages. Their initial success came from recording songs with a "pop" sound and without explicit political messages. It may have meant a lot to them that they had learned "Goodnight Irene" from Leadbelly (who died the year before they recorded it), but it meant little to the record-buying public. By the mid-1950s, however, the Weavers were recording more political songs—from the Spanish Civil War and other international freedom struggles to Hays's and Lowenfels's "Wasn't That a Time!"—and providing their own instrumentation on records and in performances.

In any case, the success of the Weavers was a far cry from the notion of creating a "singing labor movement," an idea which was also filled with ambivalence. Was the idea to represent and articulate working people's ideas or to tell them what to sing and what to think? Could People's Artists be part of the mainstream without giving up their alternative ideas and values; could they reach more people without diluting the message? Pete Seeger occasionally acknowledged this problem. Writing in *Sing Out!* for example, he said "As always our job is not just to sing, but also to select and create the songs that are needed, to decide which ones we want to sing, and where and why."[32] Lee Hays was more adamant about the problem: "'Pete, what do you want? A union man to get up and sing "Solidarity Forever" before breakfast, "Roll the Union On" as he's driving his Cadillac to work, and "Long Haired Preachers Come Out Every Night" while he's eating his $4.00 lunch at the union cafeteria?' That would be a dull life indeed if workers didn't know anything but labor songs. One of the things workers have fought for was to have TV's and radios so they could have the culture of the country and the whole world."[33]

Stuart Hall brings the problem into focus in his discussion of "the popular." Hall argues that the analytical problem arises because we tend to think of cultural forms as whole and coherent, either wholly corrupt or wholly authentic, when in fact they are deeply contradictory. "If the forms of provided commercial popular culture are not purely manipulative, then it is because, alongside the false appeals, the foreshortenings, the trivialisation and shortcircuits, there are also elements of recognition and identification, something approaching a recreation of recognisable experiences and attitudes to which people are responding."[34]

Simon Frith illuminates these contradictions in his discussion of the "sound effects" of music. Since the music industry became centralized and commercialized with the rise of Tin Pan Alley and the emergence of the mass media, the crucial cultural arguments about popular music have concerned the meanings and effects of "mass culture." Frith rejects the conclusions of the Frankfurt school theorists who contrasted "art" with "mass culture." They argued that art was a utopian protest against reality, a source of hope, an inspiration to the struggle for social change, while mass culture settled with reality, corrupting its imaginative base and rendering its consumers impotent. Frith argues instead that "the artistic impulse is not destroyed by capital; it is transformed by it. As utopianism is mediated through the new processes of cultural production and consumption, new sorts of struggles over community and leisure begin. The condemnation of consumption as 'passive' is too glib. It ignores the complexity of popular culture—the 'connotative richness' of . . . music belies quick judgments about audience passivity: the music means too many things."[35]

Frith's refusal to dismiss mass culture as commodified and corrupt leads him to this question: "What possibilities of expression are *opened* to musicians, or musical communities," by the music's status as a mass medium? Capital may try to control the use of music, argues Frith—for example, by attempting to confine it to a particular definition of entertainment or to freeze the audience into a series of market tastes—but it cannot *determine* its meaning.[36]

In a similar vein Ian Watson asks whether forms of mass entertainment can act as vehicles for spreading elements of a democratic and socialist culture. He argues that simply because it is consumed or enjoyed by the working majority of the population, mass commodity culture *can* offer possible forms for alternative cultural practice. Simon Frith concludes that the production and distribution of music are contradictory processes which are affected by the active nature of consumers. The music is given meaning by consumers who use it for their own purposes: "People are inspired by their records to make music—to speak—for themselves."[37] Mass culture is a contradictory arena; whether it controls people, gaining their consent to dominant values, or inspires them to opposition depends on their interactions with it within a broader context.

The popularization and commercial success of folk-style songs in the 1960s coincided with the politicization of U.S. society. The music was reaching a broader, more aware audience. The commercial success of folk songs depended on breaking down regional, cultural, and stylistic barriers, making Appalachian, black, and international folk music accessible to a mass audience. The idea that people could make their own music spread, and the sales of guitars and banjos increased dramatically. Social and political content in the lyrics of popular songs gained wider acceptance. Folk music even set standards for other types of music; for example, some early rock music measured itself against the supposedly authentic, noncommercial nature of folk music. But what meaning did the songs convey as part of mass culture? Did they have any lasting effect? Is there any connection between making one's own music and remaking the world?

There is unquestionably a trade-off between reaching a broad audience through the mass media and the content or original meaning of a song. The question is whether the trade-off is worth it. Former People's Songsters disagree on the answer to this question—there is no simple or objective answer—but most acknowledge that the commercial world cannot be ignored. For example, there are 116 recorded versions of "The Hammer Song." Does this mean the song has been particularly effective in reaching people or that it has become meaningless because of its commercial success?

Only the beginnings of an answer to Frith's question about the opportunities opened up by music's status as a mass medium are suggested here. First of all, the broader context in which songs and artists become known is critical. If the songs are connected with a broad political movement, such as the New Left in the 1960s, they will have more meaning than they would without that connection. The songs are then related to other things being said and done in the society, giving them an immediacy and urgency they might otherwise lack. For example, "Song of My Hands" may have been sung as fervently in the 1940s as "The Times They Are Changing" was sung in the 1960s. The latter, however, was distributed by the mass media and heard during a time when there were dramatic and visible expressions—from long hair to antiwar protests—that the times *were* changing.

Second, if one agrees with Simon Frith and posits an active audience rather than a passive one, or shares with Antonio Gramsci a faith in people as creative artists and philosophers, then it is worthwhile for people to be exposed to a great variety of cultural products, even if the mass media is the means of exposure. People can then make their own judgments about the quality and meaning of these works. Also, people can become involved in the fight to allow music exposure through the media, and this may lead to broader attempts to fight for democratic rights, as in Chile today. The media can help bring back to people a song that has meaning from the past.

It is the activity of artists and audiences, which is variable, that defies the apparent omnipotence of mass culture. In 1963 Lee Haring predicted the death of the folksong revival in these terms: "If the folksong revival is as immense as we are told that it is, then it will inevitably become digested by mass culture and it will inevitably become mediocre and it will die the death. It will die the death because mass culture does not want to preserve, it wants to use and use up and throw away. Mass culture wants to waste, to exhaust and then to discard and then go on to something else."[38] Haring's reified "mass culture" may be accurately caricatured in some ways, but it is not so total and overpowering. The songs survive within mass culture and within social movements, stubbornly asserting their connection to earlier periods and meanings. There are dramatic examples of this in the United States today: the success of the Weavers' 1982 movie, *Wasn't That a Time!*, the 1983 performance of "Ballad for Americans" on CBS television, Pete Seeger's continuing popularity. The success of pop artists such as Arlo Guthrie and Holly Near would be unthinkable without the Old Left's influence. Holly Near built a career on the basis of topical songs—about women, war, social justice—performed in a pop style. Near was inspired by Ronnie Gilbert, with whom she has performed on tour. Paul Simon's *Graceland* album is a current example of pop music that brings together all kinds of musical traditions to convey a message.

Rock stars as well have made use of folk music aesthetics and commitments to reach people with a message. The most prominent example is Bruce Springsteen. The contents of his five-record set, *Live/1975–1985*, which entered the charts at number one, are described by one critic as follows: "In addition to its first top-ten single, a cover of the 1970 hit 'War,' *Live* includes two separate antiwar monologues, plus Woody Guthrie's 'This Land Is Your Land.' . . . Springsteen's work is not folk music, but it is certainly unthinkable without that influence. From the Dylanesque lyrics of his early records to the acoustic narrative monologues of *Nebraska*, Springsteen has always presented rock as the logical extension (rather than a contradiction) of folk."[39] Rock versions of folk songs continue to appear. Another interesting example of artists making these connections is a group called the Knitters (clearly patterned after the Weavers), a folk group formed by former members of the punk band X. Their album *Poor Little Critter in the Road* includes Leadbelly's "Rock Island Line" along with folk rearrangements of songs from previous X albums. The lead singer of the rock band U2 explains his goal in terms reminiscent of

People's Songs: "On one hand, all we're doing is making pop music, but it doesn't have to be snap, crackle and pop . . . and it doesn't have to be pap music. I think musicians can do what the politicians can't. Even if it's just for an hour and a half, there's a unity in the audience."[40]

The salient issue is what effects songs—folk or pop, authentic or not—have on consciousness, culture, and politics. Simon Frith claims that "the bases for cultural evaluation are always social: what is at issue is the *effect* of a cultural product. Is it repressive or liberating? Corrupting or uplifting? Escapist or instructive? The aesthetic question—how does the text achieve its effects—is secondary."[41] This is reminiscent of Charles Seeger's advice to workers in the Resettlement Administration project that the main question should be "What is the music good for?"[42] In Frank Hamilton's words, "The question is, for me, can the artist consciously affect the political process? Can we change the world through songs?"[43]

The answer to Hamilton's question is of course "yes" and "no." Musicians can change the world through songs but not always in a direct and predictable manner. What happens to a song after it is written? Its meaning goes up for grabs. Woody Guthrie's "This Land Is Your Land" becomes a patriotic anthem for school children. Few people know that this song was written as a parody of Irving Berlin's "God Bless America" (the first version was "God Blessed America for Me"). School children do not learn the more militant verses, such as this one:

> Was a big high wall there that tried to stop me
> A sign was painted said: Private Property
> But on the back side, it didn't say nothing—
> This land was made for you and me.

A nonrevolutionary labor movement adopts "Solidarity Forever" while rejecting the spirit, tradition, and goals of the IWW. At the same time, "Song of My Hands" and "In Contempt" are known only to people who come out of a Communist left tradition.

How, then, can the artist consciously affect the political process? The answer is not simply by changing the content of the mass media in their current forms—injecting left ideas into

MTV, for example—as some analysts seem to suggest.[44] Although this could contribute to a broadening of cultural life, it is still, like the Soviet policy of *glasnost*, a top-down, contradictory approach. It is not clear whether the process through which people create meaning out of songs can be controlled, nor does such control seem desirable. The problem of making left culture meaningful to a wide audience is no more solved through the use of MTV than through creating folk-style "people's songs." Rather, as People's Songsters' experience suggests, the artist might start by paying conscious, critical attention to the politics of culture while working to strengthen the democratic process. (People's Songsters were too sectarian to do the first and too overwhelmed by the cold war to succeed at the second.)

People's Songsters had lofty goals and an admirable approach in which they emphasized broadening the accessibility of and participation in the arts, and making connections between the arts and the rest of life. They also paid attention to the aesthetics of cultural work and to some new and varied cultural forms. What they could not see from within the left movement were the ways in which the broad historical, political, and cultural contexts interacted with their personal lives, affecting their outlook, their work, and their potential to reach a wide audience. In a similar way, it is difficult for artists and critics to see where today's reexamination of culture will lead. Twenty years from now we will better understand the process going on today.

In the meantime, the fact remains that songs, and art in general, may be more effective than speeches in reaching people, touching them emotionally as well as intellectually. Because music is more accessible than other art forms, song can be an especially effective weapon—or "tool," as former People's Songsters would rather say today—when it reaches a broad audience, connects with other currents in society, and threatens the hegemonic process. Clearly songs are effective in providing internal cohesion for a movement culture by reaffirming beliefs, building confidence and unity, providing historical memory and an alternative vision. Movement cultures in the past—whether Methodist, Populist, Socialist, IWW, or Communist—have expressed great determination, but they have also met with isolation, repression, and intimidation. To what extent a movement culture, however strong (and however good its songs are), can maintain connections with a mass democratic movement for social change and successfully challenge the dominant culture is a question worthy of further examination.

Notes

Preface

1. This slogan appeared on the masthead of most issues of the *People's Songs Bulletin*.
2. Maurice Isserman, *Which Side Were You On?* (Middletown, Conn.: Wesleyan University Press, 1982), p. 36.
3. William Alexander, *Film on the Left* (Princeton: Princeton University Press, 1981), p. 86.
4. Lawrence Goodwyn, *The Populist Moment* (Oxford: Oxford University Press, 1978), p. 165.
5. Ibid., pp. xviii–xix.
6. *Selections from the Prison Notebooks of Antonio Gramsci*, ed. Quintin Hoare and Geoffrey Nowell Smith (New York: International Publishers, 1971), p. 12.
7. Raymond Williams, *Marxism and Literature* (Oxford: Oxford University Press, 1977), p. 110.
8. Ibid., p. 112. One could make a case that a hegemonic process existed within the Communist movement as well, but this leaves out the oppositional and class dimensions of the analysis.
9. Ibid., pp. 116, 123–24.
10. Ibid., pp. 116, 122.
11. Ibid., pp. 123–26.
12. See Theodore Draper, *The Roots of American Communism* (New York: Viking Press, 1957); Irving Howe and Lewis Coser, *The American Communist Party* (Boston: Beacon Press, 1957); David Shannon, *The Decline of American Communism* (New York: Harcourt, Brace, 1959); Bernard K. Johnpoll, *The Impossible Dream* (Westport, Conn.: Greenwood Press, 1981); Harvey Klehr, *The Heyday of American Communism* (New York: Basic Books, 1984); R. Serge Denisoff, *Great Day Coming!: Folk Music and the American Left* (Urbana: University of Illinois Press, 1971).
13. See Bert Cochran, *Labor and Communism* (Princeton: Princeton

University Press, 1977); Mark Naison, *Communists in Harlem during the Depression* (Urbana: University of Illinois Press, 1983); Alexander, *Film on the Left.*

14. Williams, *Marxism and Literature,* pp. 110–11.

Introduction

1. "Concluding Speech of Comrade Dmitrov," *International Press Correspondence* 15 (August 31, 1935), 1098. Scholars disagree about how to interpret the Popular Front. Howe and Coser say it must be understood within the context of Stalinist totalitarianism; see their *American Communist Party*, p. 320. Others emphasize the popularity of the policy among Communists; see, for example, Isserman, *Which Side*, p. 10.
2. Al Richmond, *A Long View from the Left* (Boston: Houghton Mifflin, 1973), p. 226. Steve Nelson says Dmitrov meant the broad left-wing coalitions developing in France and Spain when he used the term "Popular Front." This was different, says Nelson, than the general atmosphere of a broad, flexible approach to mass work guiding American Communists before the formal declaration of the Popular Front. See Steve Nelson, *Steve Nelson, American Radical* (Pittsburgh: University of Pittsburgh Press, 1981), p. 175.
3. Howe and Coser, *American Communist Party*, p. 362.
4. Ibid., p. 325. See also John Gates, *The Story of an American Communist* (New York: Nelson, 1958); Peggy Dennis, *Autobiography of an American Communist* (Westport, Conn.: Hill and Co., 1977), pp. 104–6.
5. Howe and Coser, *American Communist Party*, p. 386; Isserman, *Which Side*, pp. 18–21. The question often posed about this period is whether the Communists went too far or not far enough. James Weinstein argues that the Communists subordinated the class struggle and socialist goals to immediate liberal reforms, thereby making the Popular Front ultimately self-defeating. See James Weinstein, *Ambiguous Legacy: The Left in American Politics* (New York: New Viewpoints, 1975), pp. 57–86. Others argue that the Popular Front was so effective that it should have become a permanent feature of Communist theory and practice. See Gates, *American Communist*, p. 39; Dennis, *Autobiography*, pp. 104–5; George Charney, *A Long Journey* (Chicago: Quadrangle Books, 1968), pp. 78–79.
6. Interview with Dorothy Healey, January 8, 1983.
7. Examples of this are provided in Cochran, *Labor and Commu-*

nism, pp. 144–45, 225–26, 333, and in Wilson Record, *The Negro and the Communist Party* (New York: Atheneum, 1971), pp. 182–83, 224–25, chapter 8.

8. Isserman, *Which Side*, pp. 37–38.
9. Nelson, *American Radical*, p. 249.
10. Isserman, *Which Side*, p. 52.
11. Ibid., pp. 87, 94; Cochran, *Labor and Communism*, pp. 144–45.
12. Gates, *American Communist*, p. 78. Gates proudly joined the Army after the United States entered the war; he later led the fight to make the CPUSA a more independent and democratic organization.
13. Charney, *Long Journey*, p. 125.
14. Nelson, *American Radical*, p. 263.
15. The March on Washington Movement (MOWM) was organized by A. Philip Randolph, who worked closely with the Communists in the 1930s and then broke with them over the issue of opposing Roosevelt and the war. MOWM threatened to bring tens of thousands of blacks to Washington for a march demanding an end to racial discrimination in the defense industries and the Army. Roosevelt's order establishing the FEPC was seen as a partial victory, and the march was called off. In 1943 Ben Davis, leader of the Harlem section of the party, became the first black Communist ever elected to public office in the United States and only the second black to be elected to New York's city council. See Isserman, *Which Side*, pp. 118–19, 141–42, 169.
16. *New Masses*, December 22, 1942, 16. Labor's outlook and policies during the war years are discussed in Isserman, *Which Side*, and in further detail in Cochran, *Labor and Communism;* Nelson Lichtenstein, *Labor's War at Home: The CIO in World War II* (Cambridge: Cambridge University Press, 1982); Joshua Freeman, "Delivering the Goods: Industrial Unionism during World War II," *Labor History* 19 (Fall 1978), 570–93.
17. Isserman, *Which Side*, p. 208.
18. It was at the Teheran conference that the date was set for the Anglo-American invasion of Western Europe and the postwar fate of Eastern Europe was discussed. American Communists failed to understand how tenuous was their connection with labor, how temporary was the muting of anticommunism, how much power the government and media had to affect public opinion, and how much the movement's internal character affected its credibility. By the time some Communists began to focus on these problems, it was too late to save the movement.
19. *Time*, August 27, 1945, quoted in Geoffrey Perrett, *A Dream of*

Greatness: The American People, 1945–1963 (New York: Coward, McCann and Geoghegan, 1979), p. 428.

20. Geoffrey Perrett, *Days of Sadness, Years of Triumph* (New York: Coward, McCann, and Geoghegan, 1973), pp. 442, 12.
21. Daniel Yergin, *Shattered Peace: The Origins of the Cold War and National Security State* (Boston: Houghton Mifflin, 1977); Eric F. Goldman, *The Crucial Decade: America, 1945–1955* (New York: Alfred A. Knopf, 1959); David Caute, *The Great Fear: The Anti-Communist Purge under Truman and Eisenhower* (New York: Simon and Schuster, 1978). These books all discuss at length the political crises of the postwar period.
22. The comment on the "next war" is in Perrett, *Days of Sadness*, p. 424. The special issue of *Life* was extremely positive about the Soviet Union, stating that "when we take account of what the U.S.S.R. has accomplished in the 20 years of its existence we can make allowances for certain shortcomings, however deplorable." See "Special Issue USSR," *Life,* March 29, 1943.
23. Yergin, *Shattered Peace*, pp. 12–13, 171–76, 196–201, 268–72, 283. See also William Appleman Williams, *The Tragedy of American Diplomacy* (Cleveland: World Publishing Co., 1959), Introduction and chapters 6 and 7.
24. Yergin, *Shattered Peace*, p. 171.
25. Cabell Phillips, *The 1940s: Decade of Triumph and Trouble* (New York: Macmillan, 1975), p. 368. According to Daniel Yergin, by the spring of 1947 the public had joined the anti-Communist consensus. See *Shattered Peace*, pp. 283–84.
26. Isserman, *Which Side*, pp. 217–18.
27. See Joseph Starobin, *American Communism in Crisis, 1943–1957* (Cambridge: Harvard University Press, 1972), p. 198.
28. Howe and Coser, *American Communist Party*, p. 306.

Chapter 1

1. Nelson, *American Radical*, p. 57.
2. Irving Howe, *A Margin of Hope: An Intellectual Autobiography* (San Diego: Harcourt Brace Jovanovich, 1982), p. 42.
3. Norma Raymond, quoted in Vivian Gornick, *The Romance of American Communism* (New York: Basic Books, 1977), pp. 115–16.
4. Dorothy Healey interview with Malvina Reynolds, KPFK-FM, Los Angeles, California, December 19, 1977.
5. The effects of this process in Hollywood are described in Victor Navasky, *Naming Names* (New York: Viking Press, 1980). Earl

Robinson says he kept his work life separate from his movement life. Interview with Earl Robinson, December 28, 1982.

6. Interview with Ronnie Gilbert, January 27, 1983. The importance of social networks within the Communist movement is discussed in Paul Lyons, *Philadelphia Communists, 1936–1956* (Philadelphia: Temple University Press, 1982), pp. 8, 62–69, 158.
7. Arthur Liebman, *Jews and the Left* (New York: John Wiley and Sons, 1979), p. 313.
8. *The United Workers Cooperative Colony, 50th Anniversary, 1927–1977* (New York: Semi-Centennial Coop Reunion, 1977), pp. 36, 40 quoted in Ibid., p. 309.
9. Ibid., p. 324.
10. Ibid., pp. 321–25.
11. Albert Maltz, quoted in Navasky, *Naming Names*, p. 296.
12. Interview with Ernie Lieberman, February 2, 1983.
13. Letter from Jackie Gibson Alper, March 1, 1983.
14. Letter from Ernie Lieberman, June 1982.
15. Interview with Jerry Silverman, January 25, 1983.
16. Interview with Ronnie Gilbert, January 27, 1983.
17. Interview with Fred Hellerman, February 3, 1983.
18. Interview with Irwin Silber, January 2, 1983.
19. Interview with David Sear, January 21, 1983. Sear says his experience at Camp Wo-Chi-Ca gave him a lifelong aversion to Communism.
20. Interview with Earl Robinson, December 28, 1982.
21. Interview with Waldemar Hille, January 6, 1983.
22. Interview with Pete Seeger, May 26, 1983.
23. Ibid.; Jim Capaldi, "Wasn't That a Time! A Conversation with Lee Hays," *Sing Out!* 28 (September-October 1980), 2.
24. Letter from Mario Casetta, October 24, 1982; Interview with Mario Casetta, January 5, 1983.
25. Letter from Frank Hamilton, July 10, 1982.
26. My parents told me they learned this song as children in the 1930s.

Chapter 2

1. Howe and Coser, *American Communist Party*, pp. 178–79, 256–57, 302–3; Daniel Aaron, *Writers on the Left* (New York: Avon Books, 1961), pp. 154, 294–97; Walter Rideout, *The Radical Novel in the United States 1900–1954* (Cambridge: Harvard University Press, 1956), pp. 144–50, 166–69. The bias toward high culture, especially literature, is evident in the *New Masses*.

2. See Joseph Freeman's critical introduction to the anthology *Proletarian Literature in the United States*, ed. Granville Hicks, Joseph North, et al. (New York: International Publishers, 1935), pp. 27–28. Freeman says, "A literary congress was possible in this country only when the dichotomy between poetry and politics had vanished, and art and life were fused."
3. George Sklar and Albert Maltz, "The Need for a Workers' Theatre," *Daily Worker*, December 16, 1933, 7.
4. Gerald Rabkin, *Drama and Commitment* (Bloomington: Indiana University Press, 1964), chapter 3. Rabkin says that Theatre Union had such a difficult time finding good scripts that most of them had to come from within.
5. Alexander, *Film on the Left*, pp. 21, 35, 89. Film is a closer parallel to music because it received less attention from the party than did literature or drama. Filmmakers and musicians seemed to share the same outlook on their work.
6. A good example of politics dominating aesthetics is *Marching! Marching!*, which won a *New Masses* prize for the best proletarian novel in 1935. See Aaron, *Writers on the Left*, p. 316; Rideout, *Radical Novel*, p. 238. For the origins of "art as a weapon" in the United States, see Eric Homberger, "Proletarian Literature and the John Reed Clubs, 1929–1935," *Journal of American Studies* 13 (August 1979), 232. The social commitment of artists is discussed in Aaron, *Writers on the Left*, p. 407; Rideout, *Radical Novel*, pp. 287–89; Warren I. Susman, "The Thirties," in *The Development of an American Culture*, ed. Stanley Coben and Lorman Ratner (Englewood Cliffs, N.J.: Prentice-Hall, 1970), pp. 179–218. Susman claims that the ideas of "culture" and "commitment" were discovered in the 1930s and affected later decades.
7. Aaron, *Writers on the Left*, p. 396.
8. Ibid., p. 151.
9. Rideout, *Radical Novel*, pp. 128–144; Members of the Workers Film and Photo League, for example, "identified themselves as part of a mass of people who were eagerly taking part in an exciting new kind of cultural ferment." Alexander, *Film on the Left*, p. 18.
10. Interview with Ernie Lieberman, February 2, 1983. Jessica Mitford explains that she thought the song was "It's a fine old conflict." See Jessica Mitford, *A Fine Old Conflict* (New York: Alfred A. Knopf, 1977), p. 3.
11. Workers' Music League, *Workers' Songbook*, New York, 1934.

This book may be found in the People's Songs Library Collection, Wayne State Archives of Labor History and Urban Affairs, Detroit, Michigan.

12. Charles Seeger, quoted in David King Dunaway, "Unsung Songs of Protest: The Composers Collective of New York," *New York Folklore* 5 (Summer 1979), 2. See also Richard A. Reuss, "Folk Music and Social Conscience: The Musical Odyssey of Charles Seeger," *Western Folklore* 38 (October 1979), 221–38.
13. Charles Seeger, "On Proletarian Music," *Modern Music* 11 (March-April 1934), 121; Carl Sands [Charles Seeger], "A Program for Proletarian Composers," *Daily Worker*, January 16, 1934, 5.
14. Seeger, "Proletarian Music," 121–27.
15. Sands, "Program."
16. Dunaway, "Unsung Songs," 9–13; Richard A. Reuss, "The Roots of American Left-Wing Interest in Folksong," *Labor History* 12 (Spring 1971), 272; Barbara Zuck, *A History of Musical Americanism* (Ann Arbor: UMI Research Press, 1980), pp. 126–34.
17. Interview with Earl Robinson, December 28, 1982.
18. Elie Siegmeister, *Music Lover's Handbook* (New York: William Morrow, 1943), pp. 681–82.
19. David King Dunaway, "Charles Seeger and Carl Sands: The Composers' Collective Years," *Ethnomusicology* 24 (May 1980), 160.
20. Foreword to Workers' Music League, *Workers' Songbook*.
21. L. E. Swift, "The Return of Hanns Eisler," *Daily Worker*, October 2, 1935, 5.
22. Howe and Coser, *American Communist Party*, p. 326.
23. According to Maurice Isserman, "Browder's strength as leader lay in his skill as a tactician, as shaped by a driving personal ambition." Browder wanted to be the leader of a national movement with power and influence of its own. The Popular Front gave him an opportunity to institute a number of innovations that expressed his own political leanings and enhanced his own power. See Isserman, *Which Side*, pp. 8–9.
24. Charney, *Long Journey*, pp. 42–43, 60.
25. Ibid., pp. 60–61.
26. Alexander, *Film on the Left*, p. 91. The call to the Second American Writers Congress in 1937, in contrast with the first one in 1935, was not dominated by revolutionary language and the names of party politicians and intellectuals. The call, and the conference itself, instead were dominated by the theme of combatting fascism. See Klehr, *Heyday*, p. 354.

27. Rabkin, *Drama and Commitment;* Alexander, *Film on the Left*, p. 91.
28. Botkin, quoted in *Fighting Words*, ed. Donald Ogden Stewart (New York: Harcourt, Brace, 1940), pp. 11–12, 18.
29. Mike Gold, "Change the World!" *Daily Worker*, January 2, 1933, 5.
30. Interview with Irwin Silber, January 2, 1983; Richard A. Reuss, *American Folklore and Left-Wing Politics: 1927–1957* (Ph.D. dissertation, Indiana University, 1971), pp. 184–87.
31. *FDR and the Arts: The WPA Arts Projects*, New York Public Library exhibit, New York City, February 1983; Zuck, *Musical Americanism*, p. 160.
32. Harold Clurman, *The Fervent Years* (New York: Hill and Wang, 1957), p. 150.
33. Joe Klein, *Woody Guthrie, A Life* (New York: Alfred A. Knopf, 1980), p. 146. The enthusiasm and optimism of Popular Front artists is commented on in many places. See for example Susman, "The Thirties," p. 206. The Popular Front approach to and effect on American culture is criticized in Robert Warshow, *The Immediate Experience* (Garden City, N.Y.: Doubleday, 1962) and Howe and Coser, *American Communist Party*. Although these critics focus on literature, Howe and Coser also comment on "the cult of city-made folk dancing and singing," p. 366. See Reuss, *American Folklore*, pp. 68–84, on the Soviet shift to an interest in folklore.
34. Seeger, quoted in Zuck, *Musical Americanism*, p. 139. In 1941 Seeger became chief of the Music Division of the Pan American Union, where he worked to improve international understanding through the dissemination of music. His successes included getting folk and Latin American music into the nation's school programs.
35. Reuss, *American Folklore*, pp. 163–64.
36. Alan Lomax, quoted in "The Folksong Revival: A Symposium," *New York Folklore Quarterly* 19 (June 1963), 121–22.
37. Gene Bluestein, *The Voice of the Folk: Folklore and American Literary Theory* (Boston: University of Massachusetts Press, 1972), pp. 105, 110–11.
38. Robinson, quoted in Stewart, *Fighting Words*, p. 24.
39. Elie Siegmeister, *Music and Society* (New York: Critics Group Press, 1938), pp. 58–59.
40. Reuss, "Folk Music and Social Conscience," p. 233.
41. Robinson is quoted in Stewart, *Fighting Words*, p. 28.
42. "What Is Americanism? A Symposium on Marxism and the

American Tradition," *Partisan Review and Anvil* 3 (April 1936), 3, 4.

43. "Music for the People," *People's World*, July 19, 1940, 5.
44. Interview with Earl Robinson, December 28, 1982.
45. Klein, *Woody Guthrie*, p. 121.
46. Letter from Frank Hamilton, July 10, 1982.
47. Interviews with Earl Robinson, December 28, 1982, and Pete Seeger, May 26, 1983.
48. Interview with Ben Dobbs, January 9, 1983.
49. Interview with Ronnie Gilbert, January 27, 1983.
50. Interviews with Jerry Silverman, January 25, 1983, and Irwin Silber, January 2, 1983.
51. Klein, *Woody Guthrie*, p. 164. Guthrie's symbolic importance to the Left is discussed in Richard A. Reuss, "Woody Guthrie and His Folk Tradition," *Journal of American Folklore* 83 (January-March 1970), 21–32.
52. Interview with Jerry Silverman, January 25, 1983.
53. Interview with Ernie Lieberman, February 2, 1983.
54. Capaldi, "A Conversation with Lee Hays," 3.
55. Frank Adams with Myles Horton, *Unearthing Seeds of Fire: The Idea of Highlander* (Winston-Salem, N.C.: John F. Blair, 1975), p. 72. Other works on the southern labor schools include Raymond and Charlotte Koch, *Educational Commune: The Story of Commonwealth College* (New York: Schocken Books, 1972), and Thomas Bledsoe, *Or We'll All Hang Separately: The Highlander Idea* (Boston: Beacon Press, 1969).
56. Interview with Pete Seeger, May 26, 1983; David King Dunaway, *How Can I Keep from Singing: Pete Seeger* (New York: McGraw-Hill, 1981).
57. Ibid.
58. Interview with Ronnie Gilbert, January 27, 1983. Gilbert emphasizes that this was only true until she was about fourteen years old.
59. Interview with Jerry Silverman, January 25, 1983.
60. See chapter 4 of this work for People's Songs' view of the difference between political speeches and songs, and chapter 6 for their excitement about the hootenanny as a way to reach people.
61. Interview with Dorothy Healey, January 8, 1983.
62. Charney, *Long Journey*, p. 77.
63. Interview with Ronnie Gilbert, January 27, 1983.
64. Interview with Ernie Lieberman, February 2, 1983.
65. Michael Harrington, *The Vast Majority* (New York: Simon and Schuster, 1977), p. 175.

Chapter 3

1. Isserman, *Which Side*, pp. 21–22. Cultural influence was also visible, for example, during the CIO organizing drives of the 1930s.
2. Interview with Earl Robinson, December 28, 1982.
3. James Wechsler, quoted in Isserman, *Which Side*, p. 36.
4. Interview with Ernie Lieberman, February 2, 1983. Similar transitions from confusion to support for the war effort were commented on by David Sear, Jerry Silverman, and Irwin Silber.
5. Reuss, *American Folklore*, p. 201.
6. People's Songs' outlook is discussed in detail in chapter 4. The similarity in ideas is summarized in People's Songs' statement that "It is not very difficult to give the people what they already own." Clearly the point was not only to revive the folk heritage but to use it for explicitly political purposes.
7. *A Treasury of American Folklore*, ed. B. A. Botkin (New York: Crown Publishers, 1944), pp. xxv–xxvi.
8. *Songs For John Doe*, Keynote 102, June 1941.
9. Ibid.
10. Hays's memory of the Almanacs' travels may not be accurate, yet the point about the timing of the group's change in repertoire remains. See Capaldi, "A Conversation with Lee Hays," 5.
11. *Dear Mr. President*, Keynote 111, May 1942.
12. "Singers on New Morale Show Also Warbled for Communists," *New York World-Telegram*, February 17, 1942, 3; Robert J. Stephens, "'Peace' Choir Changes Tune," *New York Post*, February 17, 1942, 1. The major 1943 article was Jess Stearn, "OWI Singers Change Their Political Tune," *New York World-Telegram*, January 4, 1943, 1. This story was picked up by many local newspapers, including the *New York Times*, in which it appeared as "OWI Plows Under the Almanac Singers," January 5, 9. It was also carried by some out-of-town papers; see, for example, "U.S. Defamers Yodel for OWI," *Chicago Daily Tribune*, January 5, 1943, and "Four Almanacs Washed Up As OWI Singers," *Los Angeles Times Herald*, January 6, 1943, 1. Attacks on the Almanacs are discussed in Reuss, *American Folklore*, pp. 237–39, and Dunaway, *Pete Seeger*, p. 102.
13. "Hard Hitting Songs by Hard Hit People," *The Clipper* 2 (September 1941), 6.
14. Reuss, *American Folklore*, p. 229; Dunaway, *Pete Seeger*, p. 86. The song was produced by the Almanac Singers and is on file at the Library of Congress.
15. Capaldi, "A Conversation with Lee Hays," 4.

16. Woody Guthrie, letter to Marjorie Guthrie, November 17, 1942. This letter is in the Woody Guthrie Collection in New York.
17. Pete Seeger, as quoted in Reuss, *American Folklore*, p. 238. Reuss argues that a major reason for the Almanacs' decline was "the Communist movement's own unwillingness to support the Almanacs in the pinch."
18. *Bulletin* 3 (November 1948), 9.
19. Interviews with Ernie Lieberman, February 2, 1983, and Jerry Silverman, January 25, 1983. David Sear and Irwin Silber, among others, were similarly affected.
20. Interview with Mario Casetta, January 5, 1983.
21. Interview with David Sear, January 21, 1983.
22. Interview with Ernie Lieberman, February 2, 1983.
23. Ibid.
24. Interview with Fred Hellerman, February 3, 1983.
25. Interview with Pete Seeger, May 26, 1983.
26. Interview with Ronnie Gilbert, January 27, 1983.
27. Interview with Waldemar Hille, January 6, 1983.
28. Isserman, *Which Side*, pp. 1–2.
29. Howe and Coser, *American Communist Party*, p. 425.
30. Interview with Pete Seeger, May 26, 1983.
31. "Paul Robeson Says: There's Solidarity in People's Song," *People's World*, May 23, 1941, 5. Samuel Putnam mused that maybe the resurgence of the square dance was "a little of that old cooperative good neighbor spirit of the frontier coming back again" (Samuel Putnam, "Collective Spirit Brings Back the Square Dance," *Daily Worker*, November 23, 1942, 7). *New Masses* printed a rave review of a concert called "Music at Work," in which "Earl Robinson and Woody Guthrie . . . seemed to step out of the pages of Carl Sandburg's *The People, Yes*" (Elliott Grennard, "A Superb Concert," *New Masses*, May 26, 1942, 29).
32. Samuel Sillen, "Battle in Search of a Hymn," *New Masses*, May 19, 1942, 22. Earl Robinson's response was printed in the "Reader's Forum," *New Masses*, July 7, 1942, 22.
33. Millard Lampell's response to Sillen was printed in the "Reader's Forum," *New Masses*, July 14, 1942, 22.
34. Interview with Ben Dobbs, January 9, 1983.

Chapter 4

1. *Fortune*, December 1948, 209, as quoted in Yergin, *Shattered Peace*, p. 336.

2. Pete Seeger, Foreword to *Reprints from the People's Songs Bulletin*, ed. Irwin Silber (New York: Oak Publications, 1961), p. 3.
3. This document is in the People's Songs Library Collection, Detroit, Michigan.
4. Dunaway, *Pete Seeger,* p. 112; interviews with Pete Seeger, May 26, 1983, and Mario Casetta, January 5, 1983.
5. Interview with Mario Casetta, January 5, 1983. Ronnie Gilbert says she brought back show tunes from the West Coast and sang them in New York. She was not at all convinced that people thought they were good.
6. Edwin E. Gordon, "Cultivating Songs of the People," *New York Times,* August 25, 1946, II, 5.
7. "Roll the Union On," *Fortune,* November 1946, 184.
8. *Christian Science Monitor,* March 4, 1947.
9. *Organize a People's Song Branch,* People's Songs, Inc. This was a six-page pamphlet published by the National Office in New York City.
10. People's Songs International Constitution, People's Songs, Inc., New York.
11. This distinction came out in interviews. The more narrow view of "the people" was expressed by Dorothy Healey, Ben Dobbs, and Irwin Silber. The broader, more populist view was expressed by Frank Hamilton, Earl Robinson, Waldemar Hille, Ernie Lieberman, and Pete Seeger. The latter group all mentioned Carl Sandburg's *The People, Yes.*

    Discussion of "the workers" and "the people" had taken place at the first American Writers' Congress in 1935. Kenneth Burke's suggestion of substituting *people* for *workers* met with great resistance from writers who claimed that the distinction was used deliberately to confuse, making the demands of the workers appear as antipathetic to the good of the people. "The word 'people' is historically associated with demagoguery of the most vicious sort." See *American Writers' Congress,* ed. Henry Hart (New York: International Publishers, 1935), pp. 167–71.

    The question had been raised even earlier by the IWW. Joe Hill said in 1913, "Well, it is about time that every rebel wakes up to the fact that 'the people' and the working class have nothing in common. Let us sing after this 'The Workers' flag is deepest red' and to hell with 'the people.'" See Joe Hill, "The People," *Industrial Worker,* March 6, 1913, quoted in *Rebel Voices: An IWW Anthology*, ed. Joyce Kornbluh (Ann Arbor: University of Michigan Press, 1964), p. 137.
12. *Bulletin* 3 (November 1948), 2.

13. Irwin Silber, Introduction to *Reprints,* p. 4.
14. Interviews with Pete Seeger, May 26, 1983, and David Sear, January 21, 1983.
15. Interviews with Fred Hellerman, February 3, 1983; Waldemar Hille, January 6, 1983; Jerry Silverman, January 25, 1983.
16. John Greenway, *American Folksongs of Protest* (Philadelphia: University of Pennsylvania Press, 1953), p. 289. People's Songsters would likely have agreed with Antonio Gramsci's view of people: "Each man . . . is a 'philosopher,' an artist, a man of taste, he participates in a particular conception of the world, has a conscious line of moral conduct, and therefore contributes to sustain a conception of the world or to modify it, that is, to bring into being new modes of thought." In Gramsci's terms, People's Songsters were "organic intellectuals," articulating and directing people's ideas and aspirations. See *Prison Notebooks*, pp. 5–23.
17. Interview with Ernie Lieberman, February 2, 1983.
18. Isserman, *Which Side,* pp. 242–43. Isserman claims that when the Communists stepped back from Browderism they took a "fatal detour" off the road to "a stable, ongoing, genuinely democratic socialist movement." While the crisis in the dominant culture was based on exaggerated fears of domestic Communism and foreign military threats, the Communist offensive was based on exaggerated fears of American fascism. These distortions fed on each other.
19. Ibid., p. 151.
20. Interview with Ernie Lieberman, February 2, 1983.
21. Bob Claiborne, quoted in *People's World*, August 8, 1947.
22. Albert Maltz, quoted in Navasky, *Naming Names*, p. 288. The article is Albert Maltz, "What Shall We Ask of Writers?" *New Masses*, February 12, 1946, 19.
23. Howard Fast, "Art and Politics," *New Masses*, February 26, 1946, 18–20; Joseph North, "No Retreat for the Writer," *New Masses*, February 26, 1946, 8–10; Alvah Bessie, "What Is Freedom for Writers?" *New Masses*, March 12, 1946, 8–10; John Howard Lawson, "Art Is a Weapon," *New Masses*, March 19, 1946, 18–20. These articles, along with letters from readers, accused Maltz of taking an anti-Marxist approach.
24. Albert Maltz, "Moving Forward," *New Masses*, April 9, 1946, 8.
25. William Z. Foster, "Elements of a People's Cultural Policy," *New Masses*, April 23, 1946, 6–9. The symposium was held April 18, 1946. Dorothy Healey says that many Communists took Foster's article to be the last word on the subject. Interview with Dorothy Healey, January 8, 1983.

26. Shannon, *Decline*, pp. 56–57; Howe and Coser, *American Communist Party*, pp. 316–17.
27. Andrei A. Zhdanov, *Essays on Literature, Philosophy, and Music* (New York: International Publishers, 1950); V. J. Jerome, *Culture in a Changing World, A Marxist Approach* (New York: New Century Publishers, 1947), pp. 60, 75.
28. Interview with Waldemar Hille, January 6, 1983. Mario Cassetta had a weekly column in *People's World* called "People's Song of the Week" for about a year. Examples of other articles about People's Songs include Art Shields, "There's a Song in Their Hearts," *Daily Worker*, December 26, 1946, 4; Sidney Finkelstein, "People's Songs," *New Masses*, April 29, 1947, 31.
29. Charney, *Long Journey*, p. 51. Another way in which the CP's attitude was revealed was in the use of folksingers to lead songs during intermission at serious concerts. Interview with Jerry Silverman, January 25, 1983. See Helen Collis's concert review in *New Masses,* June 11, 1946, 30.
30. Dorothy Healey, interview with Malvina Reynolds, December 19, 1977.
31. Interviews with Mario Casetta, January 5, 1983; Jerry Silverman, January 25, 1983; Earl Robinson, December 28, 1982; Irwin Silber, January 2, 1983.
32. Woody Guthrie is quoted in Pete Seeger, *Incompleat Folksinger*, ed. Jo Metcalf Schwartz (New York: Simon and Schuster, 1972), p. 231. The same story was mentioned in my interview with Jerry Silverman, January 25, 1983. Earl Robinson and Fred Hellerman also commented on how poorly performers were treated.
33. Letter from Art Shields, September 11, 1982; interview with Dorothy Healey, January 8, 1983.
34. Interview with Ben Dobbs, January 9, 1983.
35. Letter from Ernie Lieberman, March 1987.
36. *The 1940s: Profile of a Nation in Crisis*, ed. Chester Eisinger (New York: Anchor Books, 1969), pp. xvii, 247. For further analysis of the political implications of abstract expressionism see Serge Gilbaut, *How New York Stole the Idea of Modern Art: Abstract Expressionism, Freedom, and the Cold War* (Chicago: University of Chicago Press, 1983).
37. Irving Howe, "Notes on Mass Culture," *The 1940s*, p. 269; Paul Goodman, "The Chance for Popular Culture," *The 1940s*, p. 261. There is much more to be said on the subject, but the point here is that social consciousness was not paramount in cold-war-cultural products.
38. *Bulletin* 3 (July-August 1948).

39. Earl Robinson was quoted in *People's World*, August 23, 1946. Bernie Asbel was quoted in Shields, "There's a Song," *Daily Worker*, December 26, 1946. Letter from Jackie Gibson Alper, March 1, 1983.
40. Interviews with Mario Casetta, January 5, 1983, and Earl Robinson, December 28, 1982.
41. Interview with Ronnie Gilbert, January 27, 1983; letter from Jackie Gibson Alper, March 1, 1983; interviews with David Sear, January 21, 1983; Fred Hellerman, February 3, 1983; Mario Casetta, January 5, 1983; Pete Seeger, May 26, 1983.
42. Interviews with Ronnie Gilbert, January 27, 1983, and Fred Hellerman, February 3, 1983.
43. The quote is from my interview with Jerry Silverman, January 25, 1983. The contrast between the boredom of political meetings and the excitement of singing was also commented on by Mario Casetta, Ernie Lieberman, and Earl Robinson.
44. Woody Guthrie complained about the language of the *Daily Worker* in a letter to "Dear What's Wrong Column," *Daily Worker*, November 11, 1946.
45. Irwin Silber, quoted in "The Folksong Revival," 113.

Chapter 5

1. *Bulletin* 1 (February 1946), 1.
2. *Bulletin* 1 (October 1946), 4.
3. Interview with Ronnie Gilbert, January 27, 1983. David Sear and Jerry Silverman, on the other hand, said they always disliked pop music.
4. Letter from Mario Casetta, October 24, 1982; interview with Mario Casetta, January 5, 1983.
5. Interview with Fred Hellerman, February 3, 1983.
6. *Bulletin* 1 (January 1947), 3.
7. Alan Lomax, foreword to the *People's Songbook* (New York: Boni and Gaer, 1948), p. 3.
8. The definition of a folk song offered in the *Bulletin* 2 (February-March 1947), 21.
9. *Bulletin* 1 (January 1947), 2.
10. Arthur Schlesinger, Jr., "The U.S. Communist Party," *Life*, July 29, 1946.
11. Letters appeared in the *Bulletin* 3 (July-August 1948), 16–17, and *Bulletin* 3 (September 1948), 11. Waldemar Hille's article, "On the Translation of Songs," appeared in *Bulletin* 3 (December 1948), 4.

12. People's Songs Library Collection, Detroit, Michigan. The following people assured me that they could not remember any discussions about aesthetics: Mario Casetta, Waldemar Hille, Ernie Lieberman, Earl Robinson, David Sear, Jerry Silverman.
13. Interview with Ernie Lieberman, February 2, 1983.
14. Paul Secon, "What Makes a Good Pop Song?" *Bulletin* 1 (April 1946), 10.
15. Klein, *Woody Guthrie*, p. 208.
16. Interviews with Waldemar Hille, January 6, 1983; Earl Robinson, December 28, 1982; Mario Casetta, January 5, 1983.
17. Interview with Waldemar Hille, January 6, 1983.
18. Interview with Mario Casetta, January 5, 1983.
19. Interview with Harold Leventhal, February 3, 1983.
20. Interview with Irwin Silber, January 2, 1983.
21. Interview with Ernie Lieberman, February 2, 1983. Barbara Dane also said that songs were tested when she performed. She found it frustrating that there was no group to help sort out good and bad songs; there was only the audience for feedback. Interview with Barbara Dane, January 2, 1983.
22. "Passing Through," *Bulletin* 3 (April 1948), 12; interview with Waldemar Hille, January 6, 1983. Pete Seeger adds that some songs looked good on paper but were not that good. Seeger says musicians were lucky to get immediate feedback on songs from their audiences. Interview with Pete Seeger, May 26, 1983.
23. Letter from Art Shields, September 11, 1982.
24. Interview with Pete Seeger, May 26, 1983.
25. Interview with Earl Robinson, December 28, 1982. These expectations were, of course, the same as those held by the more strictly political Communists, such as Dorothy Healey and Art Shields.
26. Letter from Mario Casetta, October 24, 1982; letter from Ernie Lieberman, June 1982; interview with Jerry Silverman, January 25, 1983.
27. Alan Reitman, "Pac Up Your Songs!" *Bulletin* 1 (May 1946), 1.
28. "Music for Political Action," *Bulletin* 1 (October 1946), 3.
29. "Eight Hours," *Bulletin* 3 (February-March 1948), 20.
30. "Solidarity Forever," *Bulletin* 1 (February 1946), 4.
31. "The Preacher and the Slave," *Bulletin* 2 (February-March 1947), 3.
32. "Which Side Are You On?" *People's Songbook*, p. 92.
33. "The Death of Harry Simms," *Bulletin* 2 (July-August 1947), 12.
34. "Union Maid," "Talking Union," and "Get Thee Behind Me, Satan" are on *Talking Union*, Folkways FH5285, 1955. The Alma-

nacs' use of traditional musical forms with progressive lyrical content foreshadowed People's Songs' blend of "residual" and "emergent" elements in song.

35. James Green, *The World of the Worker* (New York: Hill and Wang, 1980), p. 182.
36. Freeman, "Delivering the Goods," 576–77; Cochran, *Labor and Communism*, chapter 12; Harvey Levenstein, *Communism, Anticommunism, and the CIO* (Westport, Conn.: Greenwood Press, 1981), chapter 12. While Earl Browder was opposed to the strikes that broke out after the war as well, other Communists were encouraged by what seemed to be a new militance in the labor movement. In either case, however, Communists had little control over the labor movement following the war.
37. Len de Caux, *Labor Radical* (Boston: Beacon Press, 1970), p. 478. Philip Murray asked de Caux to resign his position as CIO editor and publications chief in June 1947.
38. Cochran, *Labor and Communism*, p. 271. See also Goldman, *Crucial Decade*, p. 79. Goldman says the intention of the Marshall Plan was to halt Communist expansion by reviving the Western European economy.
39. Levenstein, *Communism*, p. 224; Richard J. Walton, *Henry Wallace, Harry Truman, and the Cold War* (New York: Viking Press, 1976); Marie Seton, *Paul Robeson* (London: Dobson Books, 1958), p. 193.
40. Ronald W. Schatz, *The Electrical Workers: A History of Labor at General Electric and Westinghouse 1923–60* (Urbana: University of Illinois Press, 1983), chapter 7.
41. Interview with Ernie Lieberman, February 2, 1983. Seeger tells an anecdote expressing similar sentiments; see *Incompleat Folksinger*, pp. 16–17.
42. Letter from Frank Hamilton, July 10, 1982.
43. The quote is from Pete Seeger. For details about the pressure on the labor movement, see Levenstein, *Communism;* Lichtenstein, *Labor's War at Home.*
44. Interview with Irwin Silber, January 2, 1983. For Pete Seeger's comments on unions producing their own songbooks, see Reuss, *American Folklore*, pp. 274–75 and Dunaway, *Pete Seeger*, p. 121. See also Pete Seeger, "Whatever Happened to Singing in the Unions?" *Sing Out!* 15 (May 1965), 28–31.
45. "Song of My Hands," *Sing Out!* 1 (April 1951), 4. The song is still a favorite of many former Communists and People's Songsters. It was mentioned by Ben Dobbs, Waldemar Hille, and Ernie Lieberman.

46. *Bulletin* 2 (September 1947), 10.
47. *Bulletin* 2 (February-March 1947), 15; Interview with Pete Seeger, May 26, 1983.
48. Dunaway, *Pete Seeger*, p. 307.
49. These songs may be found, in the order mentioned, in *Bulletin* 3 (May 1948), 8; *Bulletin* 1 (January 1947), 4; *Bulletin* 3 (May 1948), 5; *Bulletin* 2 (July-August 1947), 5.
50. "The Buffalo Skinners," *Bulletin* 3 (June 1948), 3.
51. Bob Claiborne, "Before the Unions Came," *Bulletin* 3 (June 1948), 3, 10.
52. *Bulletin* 3 (June 1948), 4.
53. "The Star-Spangled Banner," *People's Songbook*, p. 63.
54. "Jefferson and Liberty," Ibid., p. 24.
55. "Abe Lincoln," Ibid., pp. 50–51.
56. "Ballad of FDR," *Bulletin* 3 (January 1948), 4.
57. The postwar outlook of American liberals is discussed in Alonzo L. Hamby, *Beyond the New Deal: Harry S. Truman and American Liberalism* (New York: Columbia University Press, 1973), pp. 4–5, 92–93.
58. Ibid., p. 271.
59. See Schlesinger, "The U.S. Communist Party"; Les K. Adler and Thomas G. Paterson, "Red Fascism," *American Historical Review* 75 (April 1970), pp. 1046–64; Norman D. Markowitz, *The Rise and Fall of the People's Century* (New York: Free Press, 1973), p. 223.
60. "Kevin Barry," *Bulletin* 2 (June 1947), 5.
61. See Navasky, *Naming Names.*
62. "United Front," *People's Songbook*, p. 62.
63. Dunaway, *Pete Seeger*, p. 125; Reuss, *American Folklore*, p. 272; Bert Spector, "'Wasn't That a Time': Pete Seeger and the Anti-Communist Crusade" (Ph.D. dissertation, University of Missouri–Columbia, 1977), pp. 42, 51–52.
64. "I Water the Workers' Beer," *Bulletin* 3 (February-March 1948), 7.
65. "Pity the Downtrodden Landlord," *Bulletin* 1 (January 1947), 3.
66. "Put It on the Ground," *Bulletin* 1 (September 1946), 11. The popularity of this song is commented on in "People's Songs First Year," *Bulletin* 2 (February-March 1947), 15.
67. "A Dollar Ain't a Dollar," *Bulletin* 1 (April 1946), 8. A special issue on inflation was printed in November 1947.
68. "Listen, Mr. Bilbo," *People's Songbook*, p. 105.
69. In some ways "peace" became a Soviet issue and "freedom" an American one. See E. P. Thompson, *Beyond the Cold War* (New York: Pantheon Books, 1982), pp. 158–60. The press began to

echo the American government's cynicism toward Soviet peace proposals. See, for example, "U.S. Views Soviet Peace Pact Plan as Propaganda," *St. Louis Post-Dispatch*, September 24, 1949, 5A.

70. "The Spring Song," *Bulletin* 3 (April 1948), 8.
71. Cochran, *Labor and Communism*, p. 225.
72. Mark Naison, "Communism and Harlem Intellectuals in the Popular Front," *Journal of Ethnic Studies* 9 (Spring 1981), 18.
73. Bluestein, *Voice of the Folk*, pp. 110–11.
74. *Paul Robeson Speaks*, ed. Philip Foner (New York: Brunner/Mazel, 1978), pp. 11–12, 131.
75. People's Songsters' views on black folk music can be found in "Boots" Casetta's column. See, for example, "Singing Out against Oppression," *People's World*, March 27, 1947. Approximately one-fourth of the songs in the *Bulletin* and *People's Songbook* are concerned with Jim Crow.
76. "Black, Brown, and White Blues" appeared in the *Bulletin* 1 (November 1946), 9. Josh White recorded a number of freedom songs in the 1940s, including two albums: *Southern Exposure*, Keynote 107; and *Strange Fruit*, Keynote 125.
77. "We Will Overcome," *Bulletin* 3 (September 1948), 8. The introduction to the song explained that Zilphia Horton of the Highlander Folk School had learned it from members of the CIO Food and Tobacco Workers Union.
78. See Caute, *Great Fear*, for details of widespread intimidation and violation of civil liberties.
79. Interviews with David Sear, January 21, 1983; Pete Seeger, May 26, 1983; Irwin Silber, January 2, 1983; Jerry Silverman, January 25, 1983. Pete Seeger's comments about the *Bulletin* are from his foreword to *Reprints*, p. 3.

Chapter 6

1. *Fortune*, November 1946, 184. For the origin of the hootenanny, see Peter Tamony, "Hootenanny," *JEMF Quarterly* 16 (Summer 1980), 95–98; Seeger, *Incompleat Folksinger*, pp. 326–28.
2. Pete Seeger, "People's Songs and Singers," *New Masses*, July 16, 1946, 9.
3. *How to Plan a Hootenanny* (New York: People's Songs, Inc., n.d.).
4. Ibid.
5. Theodor Adorno, *Introduction to the Sociology of Music* (New York: Seabury Press, 1976), p. 29.
6. Seeger, *Incompleat Folksinger*, p. 333.

7. Interviews with Ben Dobbs, January 9, 1983; Earl Robinson, December 28, 1982; Mario Casetta, January 5, 1983; David Sear, January 21, 1983; Jerry Silverman, January 25, 1983. Fred Hellerman and Ronnie Gilbert also characterized the hoots of this period as "marvelous."
8. Dickson Bruce, *And They All Sang Hallelujah: Plain-Folk Camp-Meeting Religion, 1800–1845* (Knoxville: University of Tennessee Press, 1974), pp. 55–56.
9. Ibid., pp. 60, 87.
10. Ibid., p. 95. See also R. Serge Denisoff, "Religious Roots of the Song of Persuasion," in *Sing a Song of Social Significance* (Bowling Green: Bowling Green University Popular Press, 1972); Jerome L. Rodnitzky, "The New Revivalism: Protest Music as a Religious Experience," in *Minstrels of the Dawn* (Chicago: Nelson-Hall, 1976).
11. Lee Hays, "The First Zipper Song," *Bulletin* 2 (June 1947), 11. Waldemar Hille, "Brotherhood Songs Are People's Songs," *Bulletin* 2 (December 1947), 9. Denisoff, "Religious Roots," p. 55.
12. Lee Hays, *Bulletin* 2 (February-March 1947), 15.
13. For a discussion of encampments and their importance to the Socialist movement, see James Green, *Grass-Roots Socialism* (Baton Rouge: Louisiana State University Press, 1978), pp. 153–58.
14. George Lipsitz, *Class and Culture in Cold War America: "A Rainbow at Midnight"* (New York: Praeger Publishers, 1981), pp. 204–5; Charles Hamm, *Yesterdays: Popular Song in America* (New York: W. W. Norton, 1979), p. 428.
15. The increasing popularity of folk music in the 1940s is discussed in David Ewen, *All the Years of American Popular Music*, (Englewood Cliffs, N.J.: Prentice-Hall, 1977); Hamm, *Yesterdays;* Bill Malone, *Southern Music American Music* (Lexington: University Press of Kentucky, 1979). Malone discusses changes in the music industry such as the spread of the jukebox as a form of cheap entertainment, the active support for grass-roots music by BMI, and the contract signed by small independent record companies with the American Federation of Musicians. Denisoff's theory is set forth in "Folk Consciousness as Utopian Ideology," the first chapter of *Great Day Coming!*
16. *Counterattack*, September 18, 1947, 1–3; December 19, 1947, 3–4; June 4, 1948, 3–4; July 30, 1948, 9–12; July 1, 1949, 2; October 28, 1949, 4. Tenney Committee quotes are from *Fifth Report of the Senate Fact-Finding Committee on Un-American Activities*, (Sacramento: Senate Publications, 1949), pp. 281–83. Interview with Earl Robinson, December 28. 1982.

17. David Dunaway received hundreds of FBI documents on People's Songs through the Freedom of Information Act and made these documents available to me; he also mentions them in *Pete Seeger*, p. 125.
18. Green, *Grass-Roots Socialism*, pp. 127–28.
19. *Bulletin* 2 (December 1947), 12.
20. Interviews with Fred Hellerman, February 3, 1983; Waldemar Hille, January 6, 1983; Irwin Silber, January 2, 1983.
21. Interviews with Ben Dobbs, January 9, 1983; Dorothy Healey, January 8, 1983.
22. Interview with Mario Casetta, January 5, 1983; letter from Ernie Lieberman, June 1982; interview with Jerry Silverman, January 25, 1983.
23. Interview with Ernie Lieberman, February 2, 1983.
24. Interview with Earl Robinson, December 28, 1982. Jerome Rodnitzky says the mood created by singing protest songs may last only until the record or concert is over, but "the residual effects are stronger and are not easily calculated." See Jerome L. Rodnitzky, "The New Revivalism: American Protest Songs, 1945–1968," *South Atlantic Quarterly* 70 (Winter 1971), 13.

Chapter 7

1. Henry Wallace, as quoted in Curtis D. MacDougall, *Gideon's Army, 3 vols.* (New York: Marzani and Munsell, 1965), 1:69.
2. Ibid., p. 63. Karl Schmidt, *Henry A. Wallace: Quixotic Crusade 1948* (Syracuse: Syracuse University Press, 1960), pp. 19–28.
3. *New York Times*, May 12, 1948, 14. Philip Murray and Hubert Humphrey were among those liberals who changed their minds about Wallace as being the rightful heir of FDR. See Walton, *Henry Wallace,* chapters 1 and 8.
4. Markowitz, *People's Century;* MacDougall, *Gideon's Army*, Vol. 1.
5. Markowitz, *People's Century*, pp. 296–97.
6. MacDougall, *Gideon's Army*, vol. 3.
7. Schmidt, *Quixotic Crusade*, pp. 133, 279; Walton, *Henry Wallace*, pp. 231, 331–32.
8. Cochran, *Labor and Communism*, p. 299.
9. Ibid., p. 300.
10. See the introduction to *The Price of Vision: The Diary of Henry A. Wallace, 1942–1946*, ed. John Morton Blum (Boston: Houghton Mifflin, 1973), pp. 47–48.
11. Walton, *Henry Wallace*, p. 197.

12. Charney, *Long Journey*, p. 174.
13. "Resolution of the Situation Growing Out of the Presidential Elections," *Political Affairs*, July 1953. In other words, as Lee Pressman told Curtis MacDougall, "There was a hell of a lot of romanticizing at the time." See MacDougall, *Gideon's Army*, vol. 1, p. 283.
14. *People's World*, December 30, 1947, 1, 3.
15. Louis Untermeyer, quoted in Walton, *Henry Wallace*, p. 244.
16. Schmidt, *Quixotic Crusade*, p. 63.
17. Henry Wallace, "The Singing People," *New Republic*, June 28, 1948.
18. Cochran, *Labor and Communism*, pp. 297–304.
19. Interviews with Fred Hellerman, February 3, 1983; David Sear, January 21, 1983; Ernie Lieberman, February 2, 1983; Mario Casetta, January 5, 1983.
20. *Songs for Wallace*, 2nd ed. (New York: People's Songs, Inc., August 1948), p. 2.
21. Quoted in the *Bulletin* 3 (July 1948), 2. The importance of singing in the campaign is commented on by Schmidt, MacDougall, Reuss, and others.
22. Dunaway, *Pete Seeger*, pp. 127–28.
23. Letter from Frank Hamilton, July 10, 1982.
24. Interview with Jerry Silverman, January 25, 1983.
25. Woody Guthrie, "My Ideas about the Use of People's Songs in the Progressive Party Movement to Elect Henry Wallace and Glen Taylor," Woody Guthrie Collection, New York.
26. Ibid.
27. "I've Got a Ballot," *Songs for Wallace*, p. 2.
28. Guthrie, "My Ideas." Pete Seeger agrees with Woody Guthrie's criticism of the songs, saying they could have been more serious and effective. Interview with Pete Seeger, May 26, 1983. Fred Hellerman and Waldemar Hille expressed similar sentiments.
29. "The Same Merry-Go-Round," *Songs for Wallace*, p. 8.
30. Interviews with Jerry Silverman, January 25, 1983; Ernie Lieberman, February 2, 1983; David Sear, January 21, 1983. Waldemar Hille remembers "We Shall Overcome" being popular during the Wallace campaign. Hille, Fred Hellerman, and Irwin Silber all commented on the lasting cultural impact of the campaign.
31. Letter from Art Shields, September 11, 1982; interviews with Dorothy Healey, January 8, 1983, Ben Dobbs, January 9, 1983. Their view of the campaign as a mistake contrasts sharply with the retrospective view of the former People's Songsters I interviewed, who all said they would do it over again.

32. L. Haize, "Singing for Victory," *Sunday Worker Magazine*, August 15, 1948, 10.
33. *Bulletin* 3 (November 1948), 2.
34. "Wasn't That a Time!" *Bulletin* 3 (November 1948), 3.
35. Richard Reuss pointed this out to me in a letter, January 28, 1984.
36. *Sunday Worker Magazine*, March 6, 1949, 2.
37. *Bulletin* 4 (February 1949), 2. The quote is from a statement released by the National Board of Directors of People's Songs.
38. "Tomorrow Is a Highway" may be heard on Pete Seeger's *Gazette—Vol. 2*, Folkways FN2502.
39. An eyewitness account of the "Peekskill Riot" was published by Howard Fast. See his *Peekskill: USA* (Moscow: Foreign Languages Publishing House, 1954). Other accounts include Roger M. Williams, "A Rough Sunday at Peekskill," *American Heritage* 28 (April 1976), 72–79; Reuss, *American Folklore*, pp. 322–25; Dunaway, *Pete Seeger*, pp. 13–23.
40. "Hold the Line," *Sing Out!* 1 (May 1950), 3.
41. Seton, *Paul Robeson*, p. 215.
42. "The Hammer Song," *Sing Out!* 1 (May 1950), 1. People who learned this song as "If I Had a Hammer," in the late 1950s or in the 1960s sing "I'd hammer out love between my brothers and my sisters," but this is not the original version of the song. Pete Seeger published an occasional interim newsletter on his own during the fourteen-month period between the folding of the *Bulletin* and the appearance of *Sing Out!*.
43. Letter from Ernie Lieberman, June 1982; Dunaway, *Pete Seeger*, pp. 148–49; Reuss, *American Folklore*, p. 329.
44. Fred Moore, "Decca Issues Folk Song Album with the Weavers," *Sing Out!* 2 (October 1951), 6.
45. See for example *Sing Out!* 2 (January 1952), 2, 14.
46. Reuss, *American Folklore*, p. 366.
47. Joseph Starobin, "The Songs of the Hootenanny Are Still Ringing in My Ears," *Daily Worker*, July 1953, 11.
48. Interview with Irwin Silber, January 2, 1983.
49. Ewen, *American Popular Music*, pp. 481–86.
50. The initial success of the Weavers and the effects of the blacklist are discussed in Dunaway, *Pete Seeger*, pp. 141–57; Spector, *Anti-Communist Crusade*, pp. 71–77; Bert Spector, "The Weavers: A Case History in Show Business Blacklisting," *Journal of American Culture* 5 (Fall 1982), 113–20.

CHAPTER 8

1. Hamm, *Yesterdays*, p. 156.
2. Ibid.
3. Interview with Jerry Silverman, January 25, 1983.
4. Interviews with Irwin Silber, January 2, 1983, Earl Robinson, December 28, 1982; letter from Jackie Gibson Alper, March 1, 1983.
5. *We Shall Overcome! Songs of the Southern Freedom Movement*, compiled by Guy Carawan and Candie Carawan for the Student Non-Violent Coordinating Committee (New York: Oak Publications, 1963), pp. 11, 16–17, 43, 91.
6. Rev. David A. Noebel, *Rhythm, Riots and Revolution* (Tulsa, Oklahoma: Christian Crusade Publications, 1966), p. 177.
7. *We Shall Overcome!* p. 11.
8. Letter from Frank Hamilton, July 10, 1982. The version of "We Shall Overcome" in the book by the same name credits Zilphia Horton, Frank Hamilton, Guy Carawan, and Pete Seeger for the arrangement. People's songs printed "We Will Overcome" in *Bulletin* 3 (September 1948), 8.
9. Simon Frith, *Sound Effects* (New York: Pantheon Books, 1981), p. 30.
10. "In Contempt," *Sing Out!* 1 (October 1950), 7.
11. Interview with Pete Seeger, May 26, 1983.
12. Spector, *Anti-Communist Crusade*, pp. 58–59; Spector, "The Weavers," 113–20.
13. Interview with David Sear, January 21, 1983.
14. Capaldi, "A Conversation with Lee Hays," 5; Seeger, *Incompleat Folksinger*, pp. 21–22.
15. Ronnie Gilbert says this in the 1982 documentary film about the Weavers, *Wasn't That a Time!*
16. See the notes to *The Weavers at Carnegie Hall*, Vanguard VRS-9010.
17. Ibid. The Weavers were not the only group to reach a popular audience with folk music in the 1950s. The Kingston Trio had a major impact from 1958 on, and even Walt Disney experimented with creating popular "folk songs." What distinguished the Weavers was their desire to "make a difference."
18. Frith, *Sound Effects*, p. 29.
19. Klein, *Woody Guthrie*, pp. 424–25. The Mary Travers quote is from the 1982 movie, *Wasn't That a Time!* Interview with Mario Casetta, January 5, 1983.
20. Edward Schumacher, "Music Sparks Political Protest of Chile Youth," *New York Times*, July 3, 1983, 1.

21. Ibid.
22. Ibid. Chileans have adopted what Ian Watson calls a "dual strategy," reactivating cultural life at the street, local, and regional level, and attempting to democratize the mass media and its distribution. See Ian Watson, *Song and Democratic Culture in Britain* (London: Croom Helm, 1983), p. 57.
23. Schumacher, "Music Sparks Protest."
24. Interview with Ronnie Gilbert, January 27, 1983.
25. Interview with Pete Seeger, May 26, 1983.
26. Interviews with David Sear, January 21, 1983; Waldemar Hille, January 6, 1983; Irwin Silber, January 2, 1983; Pete Seeger, May 26, 1983.
27. Stanley Aronowitz, *The Crisis in Historical Materialism* (New York: Praeger Publishers, 1981), p. 250.
28. Letter from Jackie Gibson Alper, March 1, 1983.
29. Interview with Pete Seeger, May 26, 1983.
30. Woody Guthrie, letter to Marjorie Guthrie, May 15, 1947, Woody Guthrie Collection, New York.
31. Interview with Mario Casetta, January 5, 1983. Criticism of the Weavers appeared in *Sing Out!* 1 (January 1951), 13; 1 (February 1951), 6; 2 (July 1951), 12. David Dunaway says the Weavers' manager, Pete Kameron, convinced the group not to appear at left-wing affairs; see Dunaway, *Pete Seeger*, p. 149. According to Irwin Silber, Pete Seeger's compromise was to show up unannounced (interview with Irwin Silber, January 2, 1983).
32. Pete Seeger, "Songs of Labor and the American People," *Sing Out!* 25 (May-June 1976), 1.
33. Capaldi, "A Conversation with Lee Hays," 6–7.
34. Stuart Hall, "Notes on Deconstructing 'the popular,'" in *People's History and Socialist Theory*, ed. Raphael Samuel (London: Routledge and Kegan Paul Ltd., 1981), p. 233.
35. Frith, *Sound Effects*, p. 268. Stanley Aronowitz also argues that there are utopian elements in mass culture; see *Historical Materialism*, pp. 277–78.
36. Frith, *Sound Effects*, pp. 55, 270–71.
37. Ibid., p. 165. Watson's point is expressed in his *Democratic Culture*, p. 56. He qualifies these remarks by acknowledging that the problem is that mass commodity culture functions as a nonparticipatory "consumer" culture; thus by definition its usefulness in creating a participatory and emancipating culture is limited. Instead of one-way consumption, a counter-hegemony emphasizes the participatory, accessible, and collective side of cultural activity.

38. "The Folksong Revival," pp. 117–18.
39. Ron Silliman, "Pete Seeger and the Avant-Garde," *Socialist Review* 17 (March-April 1987), 121–22.
40. Robert Hilburn, "U2: Socially Relevant," *Columbia Daily Tribune*, September 1, 1983, 20. This article originally appeared in the *Los Angeles Times*.
41. Frith, *Sound Effects*, p. 55.
42. Reuss, "Folk Music and Social Conscience," p. 233.
43. Letter from Frank Hamilton, July 10, 1982.
44. See Jesse Lemisch, "I Dreamed I Saw MTV Last Night," *The Nation*, October 18, 1986, 1.

Index

Books in the Series Music in American Life

Only a Miner: Studies in Recorded Coal-Mining Songs
Archie Green

Great Day Coming: Folk Music and the American Left
R. Serge Denisoff

John Philip Sousa: A Descriptive Catalog of His Works
Paul E. Bierley

The Hell-Bound Train: A Cowboy Songbook
Glenn Ohrlin

Oh, Didn't He Ramble:
The Life Story of Lee Collins as Told to Mary Collins
Frank J. Gillis and John W. Miner, Editors

American Labor Songs of the Nineteenth Century
Philip S. Foner

Stars of Country Music: Uncle Dave Macon to Johnny Rodriguez
Bill C. Malone and Judith McCulloh, Editors

Git Along, Little Dogies:
Songs and Songmakers of the American West
John I. White

A Texas-Mexican *Cancionero*: Folksongs of the Lower Border
Americo Paredes

San Antonio Rose: The Life and Music of Bob Wills
Charles R. Townsend

Early Downhome Blues: A Musical and Cultural Analysis
Jeff Todd Titon

An Ives Celebration:
Papers and Panels of the Charles Ives Centennial Festival-Conference
H. Wiley Hitchcock and Vivian Perlis, Editors

Sinful Tunes and Spirituals: Black Folk Music to the Civil War
Dena J. Epstein

Joe Scott, the Woodsman-Songmaker
Edward D. Ives

Jimmie Rodgers: The Life and Times of America's Blue Yodeler
Nolan Porterfield

Early American Music Engraving and Printing:
A History of Music Publishing in America from 1787 to 1825
with Commentary on Earlier and Later Practices
Richard J. Wolfe

Sing a Sad Song: The Life of Hank Williams
Roger M. Williams

Long Steel Rail: The Railroad in American Folksong
Norm Cohen

Resources of American Music History: A Directory of
Source Materials from Colonial Times to World War II
D. W. Krummel, Jean Geil, Doris J. Dyen, and Deane L. Root

Tenement Songs: The Popular Music of the Jewish Immigrants
Mark Slobin

Ozark Folksongs
Vance Randolph; Edited and Abridged by Norm Cohen

Oscar Sonneck and American Music
Edited by William Lichtenwanger

Bluegrass Breakdown: The Making of the Old Southern Sound
Robert Cantwell

Bluegrass: A History
Neil V. Rosenberg

Music at the White House: A History of the American Spirit
Elise K. Kirk

Red River Blues: The Blues Tradition in the Southeast
Bruce Bastin

Good Friends and Bad Enemies:
Robert Winslow Gordon and the Study of American Folksong
Debora Kodish

Fiddlin' Georgia Crazy: Fiddlin' John Carson, His Real World, and the World of His Songs
Gene Wiggins

America's Music: From the Pilgrims to the Present, Revised Third Edition
Gilbert Chase

Secular Music in Colonial Annapolis: The Tuesday Club, 1745–56
John Barry Talley

Bibliographical Handbook of American Music
D. W. Krummel

Goin' to Kansas City
Nathan W. Pearson, Jr.

"Susanna," "Jeanie," and "The Old Folks at Home:"
The Songs of Stephen C. Foster from His Time to Ours
Second Edition
William W. Austin

Songprints: The Musical Experience of Five Shoshone Women
Judith Vander

"Happy in the Service of the Lord:"
Afro-American Gospel Quartets in Memphis
Kip Lornell

Paul Hindemith in the United States
Luther Noss

"My Song Is My Weapon:" People's Songs, American Communism, and the Politics of Culture
Robbie Lieberman

Chosen Voices: The Story of the American Cantorate
Mark Slobin

"The Whorehouse Bells Were Ringing"
and Other Songs Cowboys Sing
Guy Logsdon